Bron Johnson

THE
WOOD PELLET
SMOKER & GRILL
COOKBOOK

Selected BBQ Recipes
2 Cookbooks in 1

The total wood pellet smoker cookbook with juicy recipes to turn every beginner into the complete pitmaster

— THE —
EST. **OLD** 1999
**TEXAS
PITMASTER**

TRAVIS COUNTY

- THE -

EST. **OLD** 1999
TEXAS
PITMASTER

TRAVIS COUNTY

© 2021 The Old Texas Pitmaster - All rights reserved.

Recipes by Bron Johnson
Photography: Humbert Castillo
Graphic design: Tori Vergara
Editorial coordination: Joe Garcia and Humbert Castillo

First edition March 2021

The following book is reproduced below to provide information that is as accurate and reliable as possible. Regardless, purchasing this book can be seen as consent because both the publisher and the author of this book are in no way experts on the topics discussed within. Any recommendations or suggestions that are made herein are for entertainment purposes only. Professionals should be consulted as needed before undertaking any of the actions endorsed herein. This declaration is deemed fair and valid by both the American Bar Association and the Committee of Publishers Association and is legally binding throughout the United States.

Furthermore, the transmission, duplication, or reproduction of any of the following work, including specific information, will be considered an illegal act irrespective of if it is done electronically or in print. This extends to creating a secondary or tertiary copy of the work or a recorded document and can only express written consent from the publisher. All additional rights reserved. The information in the following pages is broadly considered a truthful and accurate account of facts. As such, any inattention, use, or misuse of the information in question by the reader will render any resulting actions solely under their purview. There are no scenarios in which the publisher or the original author of this work can be in any fashion deemed liable for any hardship or damages that may befall them after undertaking the information described herein.

Additionally, the following page's information is intended only for informational purposes and should thus be thought of as universal. As befitting its nature, it is presented without assurance regarding its prolonged validity or interim quality. Trademarks that are mentioned are done without written consent and can in no way be considered an endorsement from the trademark holder.

TABLE OF CONTENT

ABOUT BRON JOHNSON — 7

INTRODUCTION — 8
- Benefits of a Pellet Grill — 8
- Wood Pellet Grill vs. Gas Grill — 8
- Wood Pellet Grill vs. Charcoal Grill — 9

MEAT CUTS — 11
- PORK — 11
- RIBS — 12
  - *TIPS & TECHNIQUES* — *12*
- PORK SHOULDER — 13
  - *TIPS & TECHNIQUES* — *13*
- TENDERLOINS — 14
  - *TIPS & TECHNIQUES* — *14*
- BEEF — 15
- BRISKET — 16
  - *TIPS & TECHNIQUES* — *16*

COOKBOOK 1 — 18

THE BEST BBQ RECIPES — 18

— 19

- Smoked Rib-Eye Caps — 20
- Spiced Tomahawk Steaks — 22
- Beef Tenderloin with Cherry Tomato Vinaigrette — 24
- Grilled Beef Short Ribs — 26
- Smoked Beef Brisket with Mop Sauce — 27
- Steak Skewers with Cherry BBQ Sauce — 29
- Seared Strip Steak with Butter — 30
- Seared Rib-Eye Steaks — 32
- Garlic-Mustard Roasted Prime Rib — 33
- Barbecue Baby Back Ribs — 34
- Maple Baby Back Ribs — 36
- Smoked Mustard Baby Back Ribs — 37
- Smoked Mustard Spare Ribs — 39
- Brown Sugar Country Ribs — 40
- Classic Pulled Pork Shoulder — 42
- Rub Injected Pork Shoulder — 43

SMOKED PORK CHOPS	45
SMOKED PORK TENDERLOIN	47
HOMEMADE TERIYAKI PORK TENDERLOIN	48
BARBECUE PORK TENDERLOIN	49
BARBECUED PORK BELLY BURNT ENDS	51
CAJUN-HONEY SMOKED HAM	52
ROSEMARY-GARLIC SMOKED HAM	54
SPICED BREAKFAST GRITS	55
ROASTED LIP-SMACKIN' PORK LOIN	57
PORK, PINEAPPLE, AND SWEET PEPPER KEBABS	59
JALAPEÑO BACON-WRAPPED TENDERLOIN	61
BROWN SUGAR-GLAZED HAM	62
STUFFED PORK RIBS	64
STUFFED PORK LOIN WITH BACON	66
PORCHETTA WITH ITALIAN SALSA VERDE	68
BBQ ST. LOUIS-STYLE RIBS	70

GRILLED VEGETABLE RECIPES — 72

ROASTED PARMESAN CHEESE BROCCOLI	73
BACON-WRAPPED JALAPENO POPPERS	75
KALE CHIPS	76
GRILLED ZUCCHINI	78
VEGETABLE SANDWICH	79
GRILLED POTATO SALAD	81
GREEN BEANS WITH BACON	82
GRILLED EGGPLANTS	83
GRILLED ASPARAGUS	84

COOKBOOK 2 — 86

LUSCIOUS BBQ LAMB RECIPES — 86

LAMB KABOBS	87
GRILLED LAMB LIVER	89
LEG OF LAMB	90
GRILLED LAMB	92
BRAISED LAMB SHANK	94
SMOKED LAMB LEG WITH SALSA VERDE	95
GRILLED LAMB CHOPS WITH ROSEMARY	97
RACK OF LAMB	98
MOUTHWATERING LAMB CHOPS	100
GREEK LAMB LEG	101
MOROCCAN LAMB RIBS	103
CHRISTMAS GARLICKY LAMB	104
LAMB WITH PITAS	106

Rosemary Lamb Chops	108
Rosemary-Garlic Rack of Lamb	110
Grilled Lamb and Apricot Kabobs	111
Spicy Braised Lamb Shoulder	113
Grilled Lamb Leg	115
Roasted Breaded Rack of Lamb	116
Garlicky Grilled Rack of Lamb	118
INCREDIBLE BBQ VEGETABLE RECIPES	**119**
Balsamic Mexican Street Corn	120
Potato Fries with Chipotle Ketchup	122
Romaine Salad with Bacon	123
Bacon & Jalapenos	124
Creamy Mashed Red Potatoes	125
Herb-Infused Riced Potatoes	126
oasted Green Beans and Bacon	127
Grilled Peach and Tomato Salsa	128
Vinegary Rotini Salad	129
Mini Veggie Quiches	131
Smoked Chickpeas with Roasted Veggies	132
Sweet Potatoes with Marshmallow Sauce	133
Crispy Sweet Potato Fries	135
PERFECT SWEET ENDING TO A BBQ	**136**
Grilled Pound Cake with Fruit Dressing	137
Grilled Pineapple with Chocolate Sauce	138
Nectarine and Nutella Sundae	139
Cinnamon Sugar Donut Holes	141
Pellet Grill Chocolate Chip Cookies	143
Delicious Donuts on a Grill	145
Smoked Pumpkin Pie	147

ABOUT BRON JOHNSON

Author of "The Wood Pellet Grill Cookbook", Bron has spent most of his life smelling of wood-fired smoke. Bron wasn't always a professional pitmaster. He spent years as a commercial banker, and it was his bank that would eventually lead him to BBQ. The bank held a BBQ competition every year, and as an adamant griller, Bron felt he'd be able to hold his own. Once the competition started, he was in awe of the whole culture.

Teams smoking meat, drinking beer, and telling stories. Growing up in the South, he knew BBQ, but the culture around the competition added a whole new level of inspiration.

Before retiring in 1999, he served his Country in the Military. Bronson has two sons and two grandchildren. He lives in Austin, Texas, with his wife of 59 years. When not in the backyard smoking, roasting & grilling meats, he can be found tending his vegetable garden, fishing, or golfing. Peter and his wife enjoy traveling the Country in their RV - but he never leaves home without his tailgate portable wood pellet smoker-grill.

INTRODUCTION

A wood pellet grill uses proprietary wood pellets as fuel. This is different from a wood grill, and especially a charcoal grill.

Joe Traeger is the inventor of the wood pellet grill. He came up with the idea after he noticed his gas grill was in flames as he was preparing to cook for his family. That was in 1988. Today, pellet grills give consumers the flavor of wood smoke with the conve- nience of a gas grill.

Benefits of a Pellet Grill

We already know that pellet grills can be used to smoke, grill, bake and even braise food, and with all those capabilities it's no surprise that they act more like an outdoor oven than a traditional grill. The options for what to cook on a pellet grill are nearly endless because unlike other grills or smokers, a pellet grill allows you to cook something low and slow — or hotter and faster. You can also set a specific temperature which makes for consistent, efficient cooking every time. With no direct heat cooking and no open flame, you don't even have to worry about flare- ups!

Wood Pellet Grill vs. Gas Grill

The biggest difference between a pellet grill and a gas grill: the flavor! Pellet grills are powered by hardwood pellets and thus impart a naturally sweet, spicy, smoky flavor to everything you cook; a flavor that is unmatched by cooking on gas or charcoal grills. The team at Traeger says: *"The smoke acts as a wholly separate seasoning, adding a deeper and more robust flavor to whatever you decide to cook"*.

The flavor of cooking with wood pellets doesn't even compare to the flavor of cooking on a gas grill. Sure, you can argue that cooking over an open flame like you would on a gas grill gives off flavor, but what if you could get that meaty, smoky flavor without the inevitable ashy, burnt and blackened taste? That's where your pellet grill comes in. Heat is generated through combustion, by igniting wood pellets and circulating heat through a fan system. Much like a convection oven, this allows us to set and maintain a specific temperature without worrying about the unpredictability of open fire flare-ups.

Wood Pellet Grill vs. Charcoal Grill

Although charcoal grills are certainly known for smoky flavor, there's one major difference that sets pellet grills apart from their charcoal counterpart: temperature regulation. Whatever temperature you decide to set your pellet grill to, you can be certain that it will maintain it. One of the biggest downfalls of a charcoal grill is that although it can achieve high temperatures, it's difficult to maintain high temperatures. We've all been there; you've heated your coals to the perfect temperature and before you know it, they're cooling off again! Pellet grills allow you to set a specific cooking temperature (some even support the use of an internal therm- ometer that pairs with your Bluetooth), so you can check on the doneness of your meat from the comfort of your couch. This system makes for a much more predictable, manageable and convenient grilling experience.

Overall, pellet grills are an exciting advancement in barbecuing. Most commonly known as "smokers," these grills are powered by hardwood pellets and act more like an outdoor oven than a standard gas or charcoal grill.
Wood pellet grills are one of the hottest trends in grilling right now. If you just got one or are about to, you've no doubt wondered how to use a wood pellet grill.

Wood pellet grills use real wood, all-natural wood pellets as fuel but also req uire an electrical outlet for power. Unlike propane, natural gas, or charcoal grills, burning pellets is not harmful to the environment. They come in a variety of flavors and are FDA approved.

Let's get started!

MEAT CUTS

PORK

Pork might not be my favorite meat, but it just might be my best. I have spent hours in front of my grill, prepping ribs and pork shoulders. As a frequent host of large parties, including a yearly rematch of Bad Santa with my hooligan high school friends, I had to start somewhere — and pork was a great place to start.

Pork has a salty flavor that cannot be mistaken. Though it can get in the way at times, the fat content in pork allows it to be both juicy and tender.

Pork goes exceptionally well with sweet flavors, and I refer to that a lot. Pick up some local honey; it supports the beekeepers, farmers, and markets in the area. Plus, local honey tastes better. Brown sugar is delicious with pork, too. And whenever I visit a buddy in Toronto, I always pick up some Canadian maple syrup in the duty-free shop on the way home to have on hand for pork recipes.

1. Head
2. Clear Plate
3. Back Fat
4. Boston Butt/Shoulder
5. Loin/Tenderloin
6. Ham
7. Cheek
8. Picnic Shoulder
9. Ribs
10. Bacon/Belly
11. Hock

RIBS

Ribs, particularly baby back ribs, are my best dish. If there's one thing I do as well as James LeBron throws a basketball, it's smoking ribs. I will speak in general terms when dealing with pork ribs, spare ribs, and baby backs. You want to select a cut with a good amount of fat in both cases, but it should be consistent throughout. Too much fat, especially if it is only in certain places, can make for an unappetizingly fatty bite.

We will prep our ribs the way you see them at a competition, not at the local chain barbecue restaurant. These will have just the slightest pull. To them just before the meat slips and falls off the bone. If you want the meat slipping and sliding off the bone, cook them a little longer.

TIPS & TECHNIQUES

Remove the membrane. That weird membrane on the back of ribs (sometimes called silver skin) can make them harder to pull off the bone and less tender. To get pit master-level results each time, remove the membrane.

Use mustard as a binder. Mustard works excellent as a binder for your rub on fatty meats such as ribs. Rub plain yellow mustard or another smooth mustard over your ribs before or after your rub. This will keep your rub on your meat and not all over your drip pan. Use whatever liquid you like best (including beer or wine, but not liquor) for your spritz or your wrap. When watching a competition cook prep ribs with Mountain Dew, I asked why. "It's what my brother and I like and what we had, so we just started using it," he told me. I use Pepsi; my dad and brother use apple juice. Use what you like, or see what other pitmasters are using and try that for a change. It's a great place to experiment.

Sauce it—just don't overdo it. Again, saucing is a natural preference. At parties, I always have a plate of ribs with just a dry rub. Over the years, my ribs have gone from dry to heavily sauced, and now I just use a light sweet coating. As you will see in the recipes, we also have other ways to achieve sweetness.

Country-style ribs are ribs. Cook boneless country-style ribs the same way you would other ribs. The smoked flavor is excellent, and they are incredibly tender when done.

PORK SHOULDER

Pulled pork is something pit masters love. Not just because it's easy and good, but because it typically means leftovers for days. Sliders, nachos, and sandwiches are all day-two and day-three renditions of the pulled-pork-leftover week. A good-size pork shoulder could feed an army—or at least an army of kids just back from baseball, gymnastics, or soccer. When selecting your pork shoulder—also called pork

Butt or Boston butt—it doesn't matter if you choose one with or without a bone. However, do check the fat content. You want some fat, or your pork will dry out, but too much can be overly fatty, just like ribs. The fat cap should be less than 1 inch deep.

TIPS & TECHNIQUES

Inject your pork shoulder for extra moisture and flavor. Using tea, inject your shoulder. A good shoulder will have a nice flavorful bark, but injecting will give it flavor everywhere.

Smoke your pork longer for a good "bark." The bark isn't just on trees or what your dog does. The bark is that delicious crust on the outside of well-smoked meat. The bark develops when the meat and rub are combined with uninterrupted smoke for an extended time. A good pork shoulder will have a good, dark bark. To increase the amount of bark, smoke the pork longer, unwrapped.

Use your hands when pulling the meat— it's just easier. There are some new cool claws available that can be used for pulling pork. They keep your hands from getting hot and greasy. Fact is, though, with those, the pull never really feels right. I have a pair of gloves I wear under food service gloves. The gloves keep my hands from burning but let me pull the meat precisely as I like it.

TENDERLOINS

Pork tenderloins are among the simplest smoke pre- partitions on the grill, but they're always impressive. I smoke a couple of tenderloins for my family every couple of weeks, and they never get tired of them. The pellet grill or smoker does a fantastic job with tenderloins, ensuring a juicy result each time.

When selecting tenderloins, as with most pork, the key is fat content. I try to limit the fat content on my tenderloins. A pellet grill will work to keep them moist and will limit dried-out areas.

TIPS & TECHNIQUES

If you're lazy, just smoke them. The Smoke setting of the pellet grill works great to get your meat to
The temperature while always keeping it moist. Use a reverse sear. Searing is usually done first, before cooking the meat entirely. When we do it last, after fully smoking the meat, we call it a reverse sear.

If your grill has an open flame option, like a flame broiler, use that; otherwise, crank up your grill's temperature as high as it will go.

After smoking the tenderloins until their internal temperature reaches 135°F to 140°F, sear them off at a higher temperature until they reach 145°F, about 3 to 5 minutes per side. Pork tenderloins are a great candidate for marinating. Teriyaki-marinated pork tenderloin tastes fantastic, and the meat can take on the marinade flavor in as little as 30 minutes.

BEEF

When I think of smoking and barbecue, my mind immediately goes to beef: significant cuts of brisket and tri-tip, steaks over a flame. Fortunately, with today's grill technology, all of these are possible on a pellet grill. But the dream of so many pitmasters is that perfect Texas-style brisket. We have all spent hours researching how best to achieve it: Wrapped or unwrap- ped? Foil or butcher paper? How long should it take? We also want steaks that even the owner of the best steakhouse would pay for—the smoke and the butter and the fire, all infused with the smell of searing meat. That's what we aim for in our backyards.

This is why I think "beef" when I think of smoking and barbecue. Selecting beef is made more accessible by its grade. We'll go into this here, as well as some other tips to make you a master of low-and-slow meat cooking.

1. Neck
2. Chuck
3. Rib
4. Short Loin
5. Sirloin
6. Tenderloin
7. Top Sirloin

8. Rump Cap
9. Round
10. Brisket
11. Shoulder Clod
12. Short Plate
13. Flank

BRISKET

In my experience, brisket tends to be the gold standard and the most difficult to cook on the pellet grill. Many look at the perfect brisket with reverence and hope for the day when they'll successfully achieve it. Discussions fill message boards on the bend test, the pull test, and the like. The problem with this line of thinking around brisket? Well, it's actually not that difficult to make! Brisket, just like anything else, can be perfected with practice and patience.

When selecting the perfect brisket—and I am referring- ring to a whole brisket, with both the point and flat cuts (usually separated at most butchers) intact— the key is not too fat. If you buy a brisket with a huge fat cap, you are just going to cut it off. Also, I suggest spending the extra money on the highest grade of brisket available to you. A cheap brisket can equal a tough brisket. Brisket is not a cheap cut anyway, so spend the money for the best cut.

TIPS & TECHNIQUES

Get rid of that fat cap. A large fat cap is just not appetizing if you leave it on when you smoke your brisket. Use a boning knife or whatever knife you have available and cut the fat cap down to about ¼ inch. Trimming the fat cap will decrease the fattiness of your brisket, but leaving it partially there will keep the meat moist.

Wrap, don't wrap. You choose. Both aluminum foil and butcher paper can be used for wrapping—again, it is all about preference. However, I will say about wrapping because it doesn't do it until after the stall, 165°F to 170°F. Wrapping too early cuts down on your bark development, and your brisket won't be as smoky.

If you don't wrap the meat, spritz it or use a water pan. Spritzing with liquid, like apple juice or plain water, will ensure your brisket stays moist. A water pan can be used in a pellet grill just like you would in any other type of grill, but be careful not to spill it. Simply fill a metal pan with water and place it inside the grill. Have a flat drain pan; the water pan will sit.

Let's get cooking!

Bron Johnson

THE
WOOD PELLET
SMOKER & GRILL
COOKBOOK

COOKBOOK 1
THE BEST BBQ RECIPES

- THE -
EST. **OLD** 1999
TEXAS
PITMASTER
TRAVIS COUNTY

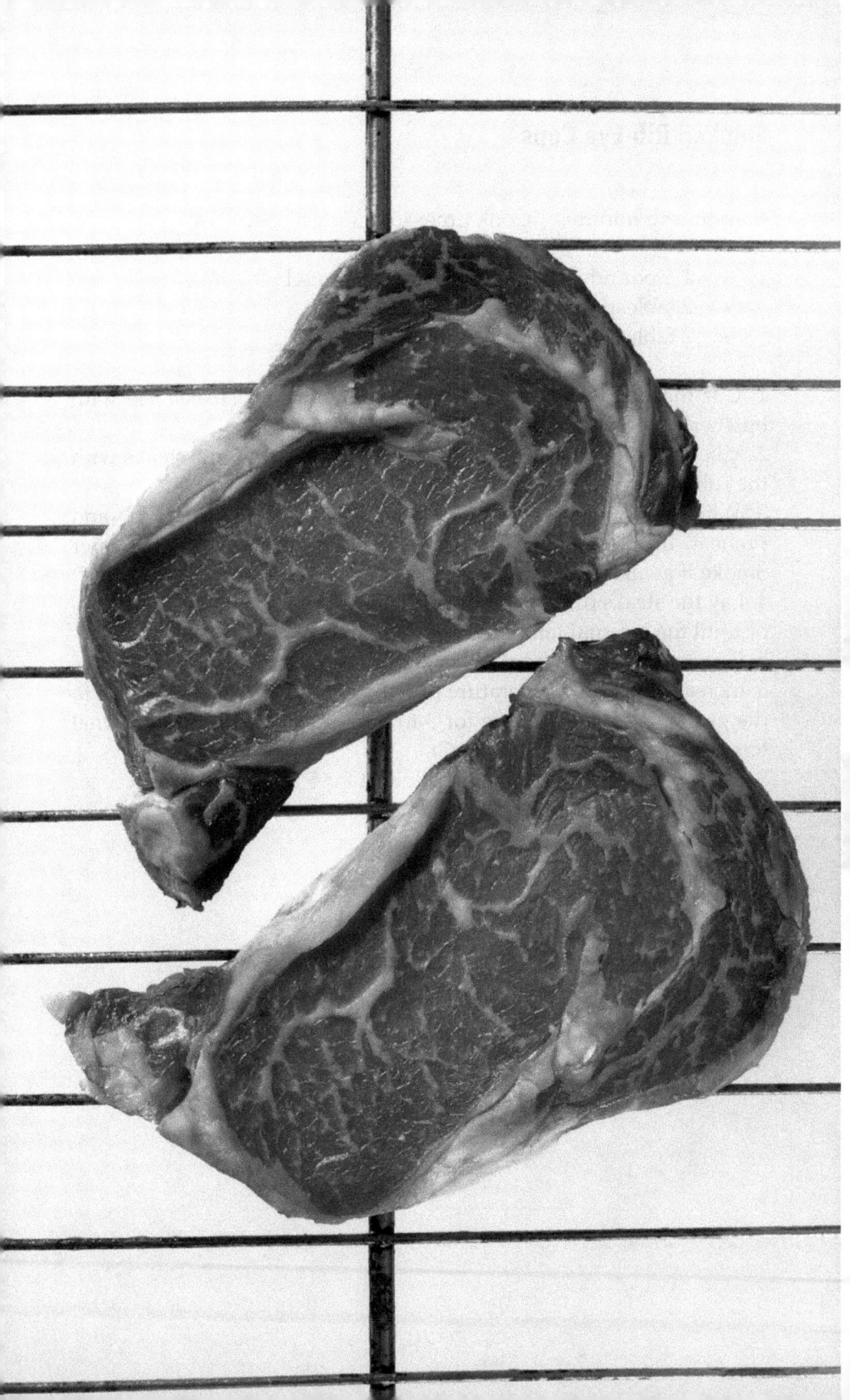

Smoked Rib-Eye Caps

Prep time: 5 minutes | Cook time: 45 minutes | Serves 4

- 1½ pounds (680 g) rib-eye cap, trimmed
- 2 tablespoons Traeger Beef Rub
- 2 tablespoons Traeger Coffee Rub

1. Cut the cap into 4 even portions and roll into steaks. Tie with butcher's twine to secure.
2. Mix both rubs in a small bowl, then lightly season the steaks with the rub mixture.
3. When ready to cook, set wood pellet grill to 225°F (107°C) and preheat, lid closed for 15 minutes. For optimal flavor, use Super Smoke if available.
4. Lay the steaks directly on the grill and smoke for 30 to 45 minutes, or until the internal temperature reaches 120°F (49°C).
5. Remove the steaks from the grill and set aside to rest.
6. Increase the grill temperature to 450°F (232°C). Return the steaks to the grill and cook each side for 3 to 4 minutes, or until the internal temperature reaches 130°F (54°C).
7. Remove the steaks from the grill. Rest for 5 minutes and serve.

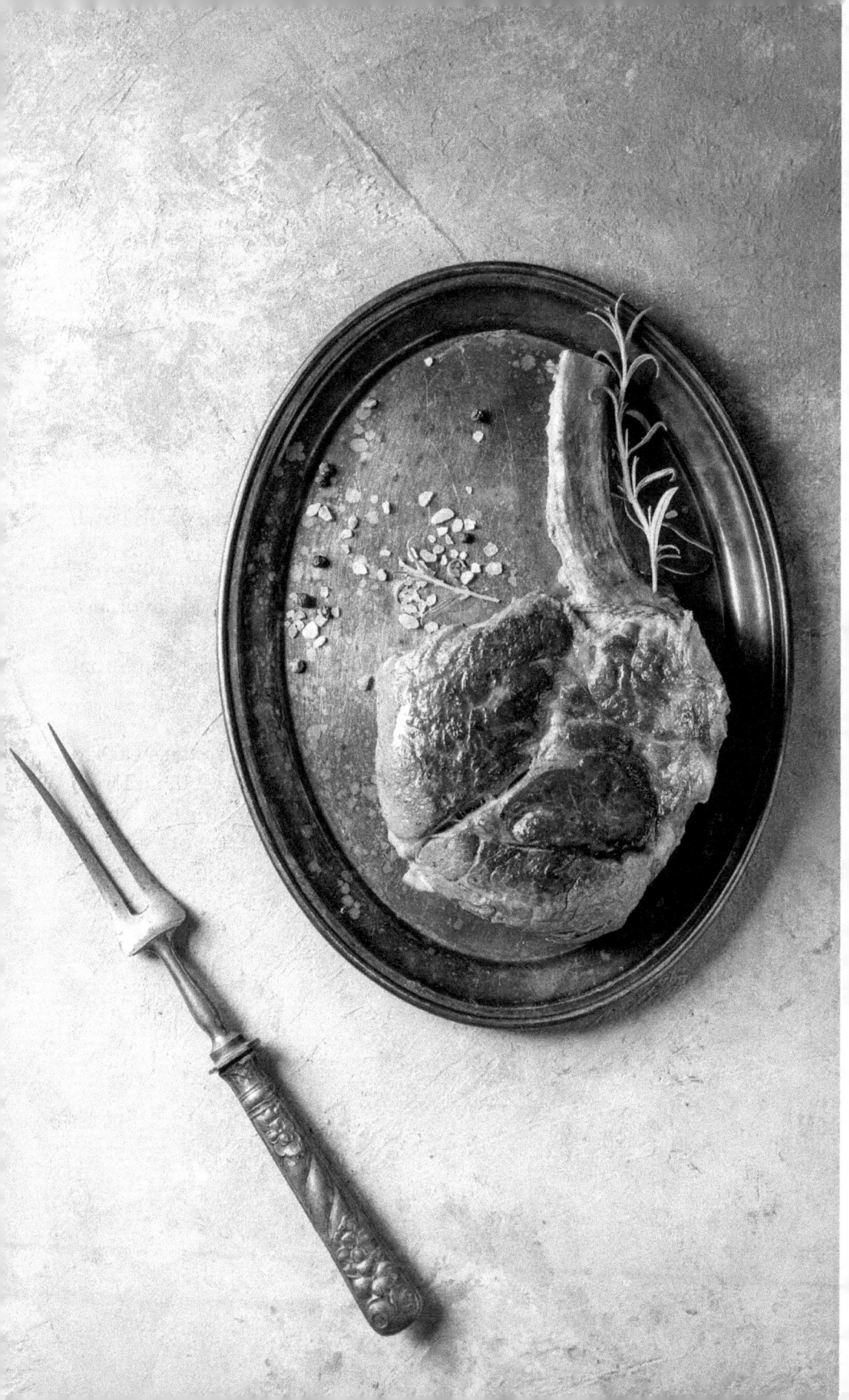

Spiced Tomahawk Steaks

- Prep time: 5 minutes | Cook time: 1 hour | Serves 4
- 2 tablespoons ground black pepper
- 2 tablespoons kosher salt
- 1 tablespoon paprika
- ½ tablespoon brown sugar
- ½ tablespoon onion powder ½ tablespoon garlic powder
- 1 teaspoon ground mustard
- ¼ teaspoon cayenne pepper
- 2 large Tomahawk steaks

1. Stir together all the ingredients except the steaks in a small bowl. Liberally season the steaks with the rub mixture.
2. When ready to cook, set wood pellet grill temperature to 225°F (107°C) and preheat, lid closed for 15 minutes. For optimal flavor, use Super Smoke if available.
3. Arrange the steaks directly on the grill and smoke until the internal temperature reaches 120°F (49°C), 45 minutes to 1 hour.
4. Remove the steaks from the grill and set aside to rest.
5. Increase the grill temperature to 450°F (232°C). Return the steaks to the grill and cook each side for 7 to 10 minutes, or until the internal temperature registers 130°F (54°C).
6. Remove the steaks from the grill cool for 5 minutes before serving.

Beef Tenderloin with Cherry Tomato Vinaigrette

Prep time: 10 minutes | Cook time: 40 minutes | Serves 6

- 1 whole beef tenderloin
- Extra-virgin olive oil, as needed
- 1 bottle Traeger Prime Rib Rub
- Salt and pepper, to taste Vinaigrette:
- 6 whole plum tomatoes
- 2 tablespoons balsamic vinegar 1 teaspoon thyme, minced

1. When ready to cook, set the temperature to 450°F (232°C) and preheat, lid closed for 15 minutes.
2. Tuck the thin end of the tenderloin underneath the roast and secure it with butcher's string. Rub the tenderloin with olive oil and season both sides with Prime Rib Rub or salt and pepper. Put the tenderloin on a rack in a shallow roasting pan.
3. Place the pan with the tenderloin on the preheated grill and roast for 20 minutes.
4. Adjust the temperature to 350°F (177°C) and roast for an additional 20 minutes until cooked to the desired doneness, 130°F (54°C) for medium rare, 140°F (60°C) for medium or 150°F (66°C) for well done.
5. Meanwhile, make the vinaigrette by combining the tomatoes, balsamic vinegar, olive oil, and thyme in a food processor. Pulse until smoothly puréed. Season with Prime Rib Rub or salt and pepper to taste.
6. Remove the tenderloin from the grill and serve with the vinaigrette.

Grilled Beef Short Ribs

Prep time: 15 minutes | Cook time: 8 to 10 hours | Serves 8

- 4 (4-bone) beef short rib racks, membrane removed
- ½ cup Traeger Beef Rub
- 1 cup apple juice

1. Season the ribs with Beef Rub on both sides.
2. When ready to cook, set wood pellet grill temperature to 225°F (107°C) and preheat, lid closed for 15 minutes.
3. Place the ribs, bone-side down, on the grill and cook for 8 to 10 hours, spritzing or mopping with apple juice every 60 minutes, or until the internal temperature reaches 205°F (96°C).
4. Remove the ribs from the grill and let rest for 5 minutes before slicing and serving.

Smoked Beef Brisket with Mop Sauce

Prep time: 15 minutes | Cook time: 12 hours | Serves 4

- 1 (6-pound / 2.7-kg) flat cut brisket, trimmed
- Traeger Beef Rub, as needed
- Traeger Texas Spicy BBQ Sauce, for serving
- Mop Sauce:
- 2 cup beef broth
- 2 tablespoons Worcestershire sauce
- ¼ cup apple cider vinegar, apple cider or apple juice

1. When ready to cook, set Traeger temperature to 180°F (82°C) and preheat, lid closed for 15 minutes.
2. Season the brisket with Beef Rub on both sides. Whisk all the mop sauce ingredients together in a spray bottle.
3. Place the brisket, fat-side down, on the grill and smoke for 3 to 4 hours, spraying the brisket with the mop sauce every hour.
4. Remove the brisket from the grill and increase the temperature to 225°F (107°C).
5. Place the brisket back on the grill and continue to cook for about 6 to 8 hours, spraying occasionally with the mop sauce, or until an instant-read thermometer inserted in the thickest part of the meat registers 204°F (96°C).
6. Wrap the brisket with foil and allow to rest for 30 minutes. Slice the brisket across the grain and serve alongside the BBQ Sauce.

Steak Skewers with Cherry BBQ Sauce

Prep time: 20 minutes | Cook time: 25 minutes | Serves 4

- 2 tablespoons butter
- 1 medium onion, chopped
- 2 clove garlic, minced
- 2 cup fresh or frozen dark sweet cherries, pitted and coarsely chopped
- 1 cup ketchup
- ¼ cup cider vinegar
- ⅔ cup brown sugar
- 1 tablespoon Worcestershire sauce
- ½ teaspoon pepper
- 2 teaspoons ground mustard
- 1½ pounds (680 g) flank steak, cut into about 16 slices
- Olive oil, as needed
- Traeger Prime Rib Rub, to taste
- Chopped scallions, for serving

1. Melt the butter in a large saucepan over medium heat. Add the onion and sauté for 2 minutes until softened. Add the garlic and cook for 1 minute more.
2. Add the cherries, ketchup, vinegar, brown sugar, Worcestershire sauce, pepper, and mustard and stir well. Cook, uncovered, over medium-low heat for 20 minutes, stirring occasionally, or until the cherries are softened and the sauce has thickened.
3. Carefully stab each slice of steak through the center, lengthwise, with a Traeger skewer. Using a meat pounder, smash each steak skewer until about ½ inch thick.
4. Drizzle the beef skewers with olive oil and season with Prime Rib Rub on both sides.
5. When ready to cook, set the temperature to High and preheat, lid closed for 10 to 15 minutes.
6. Arrange the steak skewers on the grill and cook each side for about 1 to 2 minutes. Remove the steak skewers from the grill and let rest for 5 to 10 minutes. Use a spoon to mash the cherries in the sauce. Brush the steak with the cherry barbecue sauce and serve sprinkled with the chopped scallions.

Seared Strip Steak with Butter

Prep time: 15 minutes | Cook time: 1 hour 10 minutes | Serves 4

- 4 (1½ inch thick) New York strip steaks
- Traeger Beef Rub, as needed
- 4 tablespoons butter, melted

1. When ready to cook, set wood pellet grill temperature to 225°F (107°C) and preheat, lid closed for 15 minutes. For optimal flavor, use Super Smoke if available.
2. Season the steaks with Traeger Beef Rub.
3. Arrange the steaks directly on the grill and smoke for 60 minutes, or until they reach an internal temperature of 105 to 110°F (41 to 43°C).
4. Remove the steaks from the grill and set aside to rest.
5. Increase the grill temperature to 500°F (260°C) and preheat, lid closed for 15 minutes.
6. Place the steaks back on the grill and sear for 4 minutes. Flip the steaks and spread 1 tablespoon of melted butter onto each steak. Continue to sear for 4 minutes more, or until cooked to the desired temperature, 130°F (54°C) to 135°F (57°C) for medium-rare.
7. Remove the steaks from the grill and cool for 5 minutes before serving.

Seared Rib-Eye Steaks

Prep time: 5 minutes | Cook time: 50 minutes | Serves 2

- 2 (1½ inch thick) rib-eye steaks
- Meat Church Gourmet Garlic and Herb Seasoning
- Meat Church Holy Cow BBQ Rub
- 2 tablespoons butter

1. When ready to cook, set wood pellet grill temperature to 225°F (107°C) and preheat, lid closed for 15 minutes. For optimal flavor, use Super Smoke if available.
2. Season the steaks on both sides with the seasoning and rub.
3. Arrange the steaks on the grill and cook for 30 to 45 minutes, or until an instant-read thermometer inserted in the thickest part of the meat registers 120°F (49°C).
4. Remove the steaks from the grill and set aside to cool.
5. Increase the grill temperature to 500°F (260°C) and return the steaks to the grill and sear for 3 minutes.
6. Remove the steaks from the grill and top with the butter. Lightly tent the steaks with foil to melt the butter. Cool for 5 minutes before slicing and slicing.

Garlic-Mustard Roasted Prime Rib

Prep time: 15 minutes | Cook time: 4 hours | Serves 6

- 1 (8- to 10-pounds / 3.6- to 4.5-kg) 4-bone prime rib roast, trimmed
- 4 clove garlic, mashed to a paste
- 3 tablespoons Dijon mustard
- 2 tablespoons Worcestershire sauce
- 2 teaspoons dried rosemary
- 2 teaspoons dried thyme
- Coarse salt and freshly ground black pepper, to taste Prepared horseradish, for serving (optional)

1. Tie the prime rib roast between the bones with butcher's twine.
2. Stir together the garlic, mustard, Worcestershire sauce, rosemary, and thyme in a small bowl until well incorporated.
3. Slather the outside of the prime rib roast with the garlic mixture and generously season both sides with salt and black pepper. Place the prime rib roast in the refrigerator, uncovered, for up to 8 hours.
4. When ready to cook, set wood pellet grill temperature to 250°F (121°C) and preheat, lid closed for 15 minutes.
5. Arrange the prime rib, fat-side up, on the grill and roast for 3½ to 4 hours, or until the internal temperature of the meat (the tip of the temperature probe should be in the center of the meat) registers 120°F (49°C) for rare, 130°F (54°C) for medium rare.
6. Transfer the prime rib to a cutting board and loosely tent with foil. Let rest for 30 minutes.
7. When ready, remove the twine. Using a sharp knife, remove the rack of bone following the curvature of the meat. Carve the meat across the grain into ½-inch-thick slices. Serve the meat alongside the horseradish, if desired.

Barbecue Baby Back Ribs

Prep time: 15 minutes | Cook time: 5 to 6 hours | Serves 12 to 15

- 2 full slabs baby back ribs, back membranes removed
- 1 cup prepared table mustard
- 1 cup Pork Rub
- 1 cup apple juice, divided
- 1 cup packed light brown sugar, divided
- 1 cup of The Ultimate BBQ Sauce, divided

1. Supply your wood pellet grill with wood pellets and follow the manufacturer's specific start-up procedure. Preheat, with the lid closed, to 150°F (66°C) to 180°F (82°C), or to the "Smoke" setting.
2. Coat the ribs with the mustard to help the rub stick and lock in moisture.
3. Generously apply the rub.
4. Place the ribs directly on the grill, close the lid, and smoke for 3 hours5. Increase the temperature to 225°F (107°C).
5. Remove the ribs from the grill and wrap each rack individually with aluminum foil, but before sealing tightly, add ½ cup apple juice and ½ cup brown sugar to each package.
6. Return the foil-wrapped ribs to the grill, close the lid, and smoke for 2 more hours.
7. Carefully unwrap the ribs and remove the foil completely. Coat each slab with ½ cup of barbecue sauce and continue smoking with the lid closed for 30 minute to 1 hour, or until the meat tightens and has a reddish bark. For the perfect rack, the internal temperature should be 190°F (88°C).

Maple Baby Back Ribs

Prep time: 25 minutes | Cook time: 4 hours | Serves 4 to 6

- 2 (2- or 3-pound / 907- or 1360-g) racks baby back ribs
- 2 tablespoons yellow mustard
- 1 batch Sweet Brown Sugar Rub
- ½ cup plus 2 tablespoons maple syrup, divided
- 2 tablespoons light brown sugar
- 1 cup Pepsi or other non-diet cola
- ¼ cup The Ultimate BBQ Sauce

1. Supply your smoker with wood pellets and follow the manufacturer's specific start-up procedure. Preheat the grill, with the lid closed, to 180°F (82°C).
2. Remove the membrane from the backside of the ribs. This can be done by cutting just through the membrane in an X pattern and working a paper towel between the membrane and the ribs to pull it off.
3. Coat the ribs on both sides with mustard and season them with the rub. Using your hands, work the rub into the meat.
4. Place the ribs directly on the grill grate and smoke for 3 hours.
5. Remove the ribs from the grill and place them, bone-side up, on enough aluminum foil to wrap the ribs completely. Drizzle 2 tablespoons of maple syrup over the ribs and sprinkle them with 1 tablespoon of brown sugar. Flip the ribs and repeat the maple syrup and brown sugar application on the meat side.
6. Increase the grill's temperature to 300°F (149°C).
7. Fold in three sides of the foil around the ribs and add the cola. Fold in the last side, completely enclosing the ribs and liquid. Return the ribs to the grill and cook for 30 to 45 minutes.
8. Remove the ribs from the grill and unwrap them from the foil.
9. In a small bowl, stir together the barbecue sauce and remaining 6 tablespoons of maple syrup. Use this to baste the ribs. Return the ribs to the grill, without the foil, and cook for 15 minutes to caramelize the sauce.
10. Cut into individual ribs and serve immediately.

Smoked Mustard Baby Back Ribs

Prep time: 25 minutes | Cook time: 4 to 6 hours | Serves 4 to 8

- 2 (2- or 3-pound / 907- or 1360-g) racks baby back ribs
- 2 tablespoons yellow mustard
- 1 batch Pork Rub

1. Supply your smoker with wood pellets and follow the manufacturer's specific start-up procedure. Preheat the grill, with the lid closed, to 225°F (107°C).
2. Remove the membrane from the backside of the ribs. This can be done by cutting just through the membrane in an X pattern and working a paper towel between the membrane and the ribs to pull it off.
3. Coat the ribs on both sides with mustard and season them with the rub. Using your hands, work the rub into the meat.
4. Place the ribs directly on the grill grate and smoke until their internal temperature reaches between 190°F (88°C) and 200°F (93°C).
5. Remove the racks from the grill and cut into individual ribs. Serve immediately.

Smoked Mustard Spare Ribs

Prep time: 25 minutes | Cook time: 4 to 6 hours | Serves 4 to 8

- 2 (2- or 3-pound / 907- or 1360-g) racks spare ribs
- 2 tablespoons yellow mustard
- 1 batch Sweet Brown Sugar Rub
- ¼ cup The Ultimate BBQ Sauce

1. Supply your smoker with wood pellets and follow the manufacturer's specific start-up procedure. Preheat the grill, with the lid closed, to 225°F (107°C).
2. Remove the membrane from the backside of the ribs. This can be done by cutting just through the membrane in an X pattern and working a paper towel between the membrane and the ribs to pull it off.
3. Coat the ribs on both sides with mustard and season with the rub. Using your hands, work the rub into the meat.
4. Place the ribs directly on the grill grate and smoke until their internal temperature reaches between 190°F (88°C) and 200°F (93°C).
5. Baste both sides of the ribs with barbecue sauce.
6. Increase the grill's temperature to 300°F (149°C) and continue to cook the ribs for 15 minutes more.
7. Remove the racks from the grill, cut them into individual ribs, and serve immediately.

Brown Sugar Country Ribs

Prep time: 25 minutes | Cook time: 4 hours | Serves 12 to 15

- 2 pounds (907 g) country-style ribs
- 1 batch Sweet Brown Sugar Rub
- 2 tablespoons light brown sugar
- 1 cup Pepsi or other cola
- ¼ cup The Ultimate BBQ Sauce

1. Supply your smoker with wood pellets and follow the manufacturer's specific start-up procedure. Preheat the grill, with the lid closed, to 180°F (82°C).
2. Sprinkle the ribs with the rub and use your hands to work the rub into the meat.
3. Place the ribs directly on the grill grate and smoke for 3 hours.
4. Remove the ribs from the grill and place them on enough aluminum foil to wrap them completely. Dust the brown sugar over the ribs.
5. Increase the grill's temperature to 300°F (149°C).
6. Fold in three sides of the foil around the ribs and add the cola. Fold in the last side, completely enclosing the ribs and liquid. Return the ribs to the grill and cook for 45 minutes.
7. Remove the ribs from the foil and place them on the grill grate. Baste all sides of the ribs with barbecue sauce. Cook for 15 minutes more to caramelize the sauce.
8. Remove the ribs from the grill and serve immediately.

Classic Pulled Pork Shoulder

Prep time: 15 minutes | Cook time: 16 to 20 hours | Serves 8 to 12

- 1 (6- to 8-pound / 2.7- to 3.6-kg) bone-in pork shoulder
- 2 tablespoons yellow mustard
- 1 batch Pork Rub

1. Supply your smoker with wood pellets and follow the manufacturer's specific start-up procedure. Preheat the grill, with the lid closed, to 225°F (107°C).
2. Coat the pork shoulder all over with mustard and season it with the rub. Using your hands, work the rub into the meat.
Place the shoulder on the grill grate and smoke until its internal temperature reaches 195°F (91°C).
3. Pull the shoulder from the grill and wrap it completely in aluminum foil or butcher paper. Place it in a cooler, cover the cooler, and let it rest for 1 or 2 hours.
Remove the pork shoulder from the cooler and unwrap it. Remove the shoulder bone and pull the pork apart using just your fingers. Serve immediately as desired. Leftovers are encouraged.

Rub Injected Pork Shoulder

Prep time: 15 minutes | Cook time: 16 to 20 hours | Serves 8 to 12

- 1 (6- to 8-pound / 2.7- to 3.6-kg) bone-in pork shoulder
- 2 cups Tea Injectable made with Pork Rub
- 2 tablespoons yellow mustard
- 1 batch Pork Rub

1. Supply your smoker with wood pellets and follow the manufacturer's specific start-up procedure. Preheat the grill, with the lid closed, to 225°F (107°C).
2. Inject the pork shoulder throughout with the tea injectable.
3. Coat the pork shoulder all over with mustard and season it with the rub. Using your hands, work the rub into the meat.
4. Place the shoulder directly on the grill grate and smoke until its internal temperature reaches 160°F (71°C) and a dark bark has formed on the exterior.
5. Pull the shoulder from the grill and wrap it completely in aluminum foil or butcher paper.
6. Increase the grill's temperature to 350°F (177°C).
7. Return the pork shoulder to the grill and cook until its internal temperature reaches 195°F (91°C).
8. Pull the shoulder from the grill and place it in a cooler. Cover the cooler and let the pork rest for 1 or 2 hours.
9. Remove the pork shoulder from the cooler and unwrap it. Remove the shoulder bone and pull the pork apart using just your fingers. Serve immediately.

Smoked Pork Chops

Prep time: 10 minutes | Cook time: 55 minutes | Serves 4

- 1 (12-pound / 5.4-g) full packer brisket
- 2 tablespoons yellow mustard
- 1 batch Espresso Brisket Rub
- Worcestershire Mop and Spritz, for spritzing

1. Supply your smoker with wood pellets and follow the manufacturer's specific start-up procedure. Preheat the grill, with the lid closed, to 180°F (82°C).
2. Season the pork chops on both sides with salt and pepper.
3. Place the chops directly on the grill grate and smoke for 30 minute.
4. Increase the grill's temperature to 350°F (177°C). Continue to cook the chops until their internal temperature reaches 145°F (63°C).
5. Remove the pork chops from the grill and let them rest for 5 minutes before serving.

Smoked Pork Tenderloin

Prep time: 15 minutes | Cook time: 4 to 5 hours | Serves 4 to 6

- 2 (1-pound / 454-g) pork tenderloins
- 1 batch Pork Rub

1. Supply your smoker with wood pellets and follow the manufacturer's specific start-up procedure. Preheat the grill, with the lid closed, to 180°F (82°C).
2. Generously season the tenderloins with the rub. Using your hands, work the rub into the meat.
3. Place the tenderloins directly on the grill grate and smoke for 4 or 5 hours, until their internal temperature reaches 145°F (63°C).
4. Remove the tenderloins from the grill and let them rest for 5 to 10 minute before thinly slicing and serving.

Homemade Teriyaki Pork Tenderloin

Prep time: 30 minutes | Cook time: 1½ to 2 hours | Serves 12 to 15

- 2 (1-pound / 454-g) pork tenderloins
- 1 batch Quick and Easy Teriyaki Marinade
- Smoked salt, to taste

1. In a large zip-top bag, combine the tenderloins and marinade. Seal the bag, turn to coat, and refrigerate the pork for at least 30 minute — I recommend up to overnight.
2. Supply your smoker with wood pellets and follow the manufacturer's specific start-up procedure. Preheat the grill, with the lid closed, to 180°F (82°C).
3. Remove the tenderloins from the marinade and season them with smoked salt.
4. Place the tenderloins directly on the grill grate and smoke for 1 hour.
5. Increase the grill's temperature to 300°F (149°C) and continue to cook until the pork's internal temperature reaches 145°F (63°C).
6. Remove the tenderloins from the grill and let them rest for 5 to 10 minute, before thinly slicing and serving.

Barbecue Pork Tenderloin

Prep time: 5 minutes | Cook time: 30 minutes | Serves 4 to 6

- 2 (1-pound / 454-g) pork tenderloins
- 1 batch sweet and spicy cinnamon rub

1. Supply your smoker with wood pellets and follow the manufacturer's specific start-up procedure. Preheat the grill, with the lid closed, to 350°F (177°C).
2. Generously season the tenderloins with the rub. Using your hands, work the rub into the meat.
3. Place the tenderloins directly on the grill grate and smoke until their internal temperature reaches 145°F (63°C).
4. Remove the tenderloins from the grill and let them rest for 5 to 10 minute, before thinly slicing and serving.

Barbecued Pork Belly Burnt Ends

Prep time: 30 minutes | Cook time: 6 hours | Serves 8 to 10

- 1 (3-pound / 1.4-kg) skinless pork belly (if not already skinned, use a sharp boning knife to remove the skin from the belly), cut into 1½- to 2-inch cubes
- 1 batch Sweet Brown Sugar Rub
- ½ cup honey
- 1 cup The Ultimate BBQ Sauce
- 2 tablespoons light brown sugar

1. Supply your smoker with wood pellets and follow the manufacturer's specific start-up procedure. Preheat the grill, with the lid closed, to 250°F (121°C).
2. Generously season the pork belly cubes with the rub. Using your hands, work the rub into the meat.
3. Place the pork cubes directly on the grill grate and smoke until their internal temperature reaches 195°F (91°C).
4. Transfer the cubes from the grill to an aluminum pan. Add the honey, barbecue sauce, and brown sugar. Stir to combine and coat the pork.
5. Place the pan in the grill and smoke the pork for 1 hour, uncovered. Remove the pork from the grill and serve immediately.

Cajun-Honey Smoked Ham

Prep time: 20 minutes | Cook time: 4 or 5 hours | Serves 12 to 15 •

- 1 (5- or 6-pound / 2.3- or 2.7-kg) bone-in smoked ham
- 1 batch Cajun Rub
- 3 tablespoons honey

1. Supply your smoker with wood pellets and follow the manufacturer's specific start-up procedure. Preheat the grill, with the lid closed, to 225°F (107°C).
2. Generously season the ham with the rub and place it either in a pan or directly on the grill grate. Smoke it for 1 hour.
3. Drizzle the honey over the ham and continue to smoke it until the ham's internal temperature reaches 145°F (63°C).
4. Remove the ham from the grill and let it rest for 5 to 10 minute, before thinly slicing and serving.

Rosemary-Garlic Smoked Ham

Prep time: 15 minutes | Cook time: 5 or 6 hours | Serves 12 to 15

- 1 (10-pound / 4.5-kg) fresh ham, skin removed
- 2 tablespoons olive oil
- 1 batch Rosemary-Garlic Lamb Seasoning

1. Supply your smoker with wood pellets and follow the manufacturer's specific start-up procedure. Preheat the grill, with the lid closed, to 180°F (82°C).
2. Rub the ham all over with olive oil and sprinkle it with the seasoning.
3. Place the ham directly on the grill grate and smoke for 3 hours.
4. Increase the grill's temperature to 375°F (191°C) and continue to smoke the ham until its internal temperature reaches 170°F (77°C).
5. Remove the ham from the grill and let it rest for 10 minute, before carving and serving.

Spiced Breakfast Grits

Prep time: 20 minutes | Cook time: 30 to 40 minute | Serves 12 to 15

- 2 cups chicken stock
- 1 cup water
- 1 cup quick-cooking grits
- 3 tablespoons unsalted butter
- 2 tablespoons minced garlic
- 1 medium onion, chopped
- 1 jalapeño pepper, stemmed, seeded, and chopped
- 1 teaspoon cayenne pepper
- 2 teaspoons red pepper flakes
- 1 tablespoon hot sauce
- 1 cup shredded Monterey Jack cheese
- 1 cup sour cream
- Salt, to taste
- Freshly ground black pepper, to taste
- 2 eggs, beaten
- ⅓ cup half-and-half
- 3 cups leftover pulled pork (preferably smoked)

1. Supply your smoker with wood pellets and follow the manufacturer's specific start-up procedure. Preheat, with the lid closed, to 350°F (177°C).
2. On your kitchen stove top, in a large saucepan over high heat, bring the chicken stock and water to a boil.
3. Add the grits and reduce the heat to low, then stir in the butter, garlic, onion, jalapeño, cayenne, red pepper flakes, hot sauce, cheese, and sour cream. Season with salt and pepper, then cook for about 5 minutes.
4. Temper the beaten eggs (see Tip below) and incorporate into the grits. Remove the saucepan from the heat and stir in the half-and-half and pulled pork. Pour the grits into a greased grill-safe 9-by-13-inch casserole dish or aluminum pan.
6. Transfer to the grill, close the lid, and bake for 30 to 40 minute, covering with aluminum foil toward the end of cooking if the grits start to get too brown on top.

Roasted Lip-Smackin' Pork Loin

Prep time: 10 minutes | Cook time: 3 hours | Serves 8

- ¼ cup finely ground coffee
- ¼ cup paprika
- ¼ cup garlic powder
- 2 tablespoons chili powder
- 1 tablespoon packed light brown sugar
- 1 tablespoon ground allspice
- 1 tablespoon ground coriander
- 1 tablespoon freshly ground black pepper
- 2 teaspoons ground mustard
- 1½ teaspoons celery seeds
- 1 (1½- to 2-pound) pork loin roast

1. Supply your smoker with wood pellets and follow the manufacturer's specific start-up procedure. Preheat, with the lid closed, to 250°F (121°C).
2. In a small bowl, combine the ground coffee, paprika, garlic powder, chili powder, brown sugar, allspice, coriander, pepper, mustard, and celery seeds to create a rub, and generously apply it to the pork loin roast.
3. Place the pork loin on the grill, fat-side up, close the lid, and roast for 3 hours, or until a meat thermometer inserted in the thickest part of the meat reads 160°F (71°C).
4. Let the pork rest for 5 minutes before slicing and serving.

Pork, Pineapple, and Sweet Pepper Kebabs

Prep time: 20 minutes | Cook time: 1 to 4 hours | Serves 12 to 15

- 1 (20-ounce / 567-g) bottle hoisin sauce
- ½ cup Sriracha
- ¼ cup honey
- ¼ cup apple cider vinegar
- 2 tablespoons canola oil
- 2 teaspoons minced garlic
- 2 teaspoons onion powder
- 1 teaspoon ground ginger
- 1 teaspoon salt
- 1 teaspoon freshly ground black pepper
- 2 pounds thick-cut pork chops or pork loin, cut into 2-inch cubes
- 10 ounces fresh pineapple, cut into chunks
- 1 red onion, cut into wedges
- 1 bag mini sweet peppers, tops removed and seeded
- 12 metal or wooden skewers (soaked in water for 30 minute if wooden)

1. In a small bowl, stir together the hoisin, Sriracha, honey, vinegar, oil, minced garlic, onion powder, ginger, salt, and black pepper to create the marinade. Reserve ¼ cup for basting.
2. Toss the pork cubes, pineapple chunks, onion wedges, and mini peppers in the remaining marinade. Cover and refrigerate for at least 1 hour or up to 4 hours.
3. Supply your smoker with wood pellets and follow the manufacturer's specific start-up procedure. Preheat, with the lid closed, to 450°F (232°C).
4. Remove the pork, pineapple, and veggies from the marinade; do not rinse. Discard the c.
5. Use the double-skewer techniq ue to assemble the kebabs (see Tip below). Thread each of 6 skewers with a piece of pork, a piece of pineapple, a piece of onion, and a sweet mini pepper, making sure that the skewer goes through the left side of the ingredie nts. Repeat the threading on each skewer two more times. Double-skewer the

kebabs by sticking another 6 skewers through the right side of the ingredients.

6. Place the kebabs directly on the grill, close the lid, and smoke for 10 to 12 minutes, turning once. They are done when a meat thermometer inserted in the pork reads 160°F (71°C).

Jalapeño Bacon-Wrapped Tenderloin

Prep time: 25 minutes | Cook time: 2½ hours | Serves 4 to 6

- ¼ cup yellow mustard
- 2 (1-pound / 454-g) pork tenderloins
- ¼ cup Pork Rub
- 8 ounces (227 g) cream cheese, softened
- 1 cup grated Cheddar cheese
- 1 tablespoon unsalted butter, melted
- 1 tablespoon minced garlic
- 2 jalapeño peppers, seeded and diced
- 1½ pounds bacon

1. Slather the mustard all over the pork tenderloins, then sprinkle generously with the dry rub to coat the meat.
2. Supply your smoker with wood pellets and follow the manufacturer's specific start-up procedure. Preheat, with the lid closed, to 225°F (107°C).
3. Place the tenderloins directly on the grill, close the lid, and smoke for 2 hours.
4. Remove the pork from the grill and increase the temperature to 375°F (191°C).
5. In a small bowl, combine the cream cheese, Cheddar cheese, melted butter, garlic, and jalapeños.
6. Starting from the top, slice deeply along the center of each tenderloin end to end, creating a cavity.
7. Spread half of the cream cheese mixture in the cavity of one tenderloin. Repeat with the remaining mixture and the other piece of meat.
8. Securely wrap one tenderloin with half of the bacon. Repeat with the remaining bacon and the other piece of meat.
9. Transfer the bacon-wrapped tenderloins to the grill, close the lid, and smoke for about 30 minute, or until a meat thermometer inserted in the thickest part of the meat reads 160°F (71°C) and the bacon is browned and cooked through.
10. Let the tenderloins rest for 5 to 10 minute before slicing and serving.

Brown Sugar-Glazed Ham

Prep time: 30 minutes | Cook time: 5 hours | Serves 12 to 15

- 1 (12- to 15-pound / 5.4- to 6.8-kg) whole bone-in ham, fully cooked
- ¼ cup yellow mustard
- 1 cup pineapple juice
- ½ cup packed light brown sugar
- 1 teaspoon ground cinnamon
- ½ teaspoon ground cloves

1. Supply your smoker with wood pellets and follow the manufacturer's specific start-up procedure. Preheat, with the lid closed, to 275°F (135°C).
2. Trim off the excess fat and skin from the ham, leaving a ¼-inch layer of fat. Put the ham in an aluminum foil – lined roasting pan.
3. On your kitchen stove top, in a medium saucepan over low heat, combine the mustard, pineapple juice, brown sugar, cinnamon, and cloves and simmer for 15 minutes, or until thick and reduced by about half.
4. Baste the ham with half of the pineapple – brown sugar syrup, reserving the rest for basting later in the cook.
5. Place the roasting pan on the grill, close the lid, and smoke for 4 hours.
6. Baste the ham with the remaining pineapple – brown sugar syrup and continue smoking with the lid closed for another hour, or until a meat thermometer inserted in the thickest part of the ham reads 140°F (60°C).
7. Remove the ham from the grill, tent with foil, and let rest for 20 minute before carving.

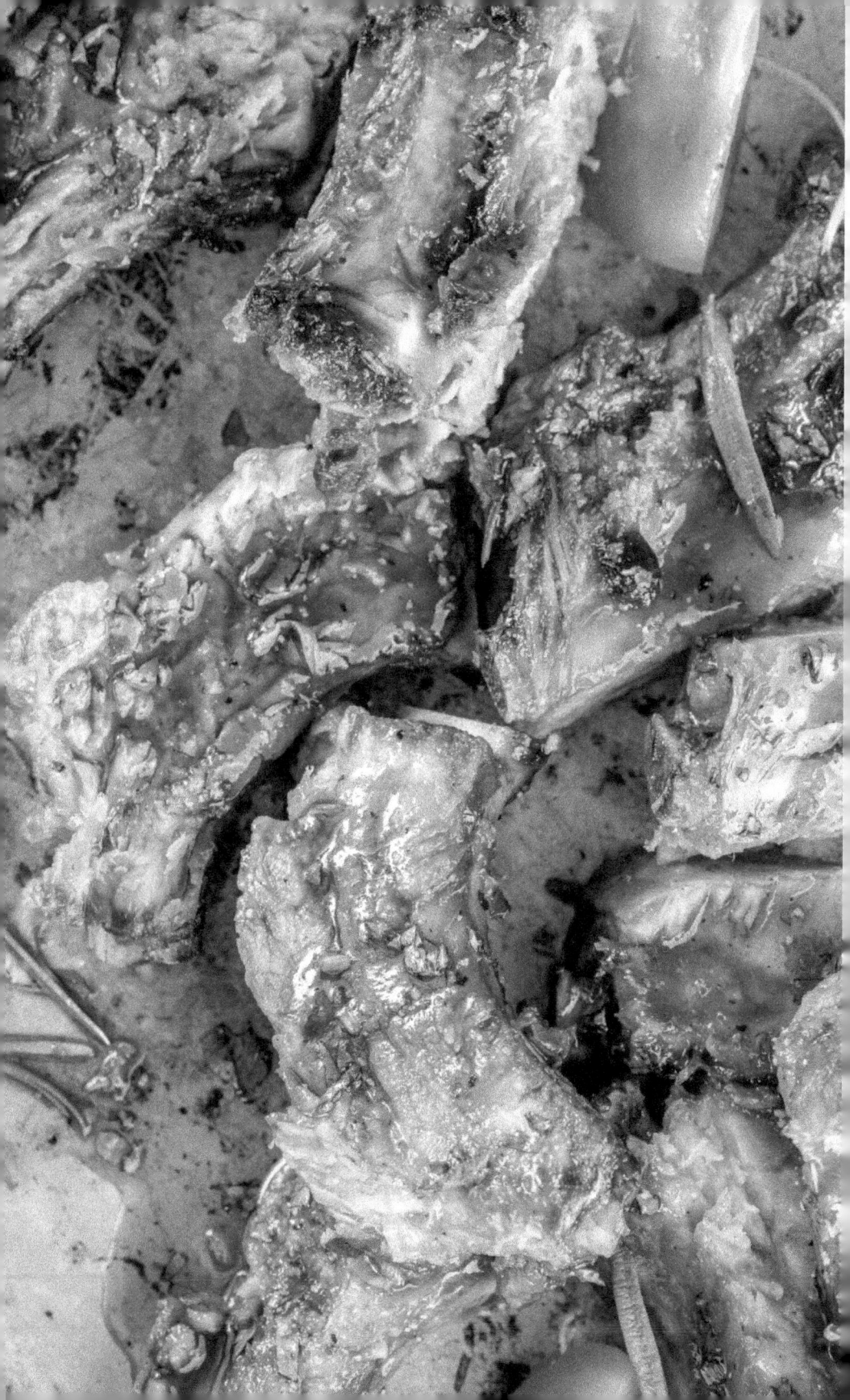

Stuffed Pork Ribs

Prep time: 1 hour | Cook time: 3 hours | Serves 2 to 4

- 10 pound (4.5 kg) crown roast of pork, 12-14 ribs
- 1 cup apple juice or cider
- 2 tablespoon apple cider vinegar
- 2 tablespoon Dijon mustard
- 1 tablespoon brown sugar
- 2 clove garlic, minced
- 2 tablespoon thyme or rosemary, fresh
- 1 teaspoon salt
- 1 teaspoon coarse ground black pepper, divided
- ½ cup olive oil
- 8 cup your favorite stuffing, prepared according to the package directions, or homemade

1. Set the pork on a flat rack in a shallow roasting pan. Cover the end of each bone with a small piece of foil.
2. Make the marinade: Bring the apple cider to a boil over high heat and reduce by half. Remove from the heat, and whisk in the vinegar, mustard, brown sugar, garlic, thyme, and salt and pepper. Slowly whisk in the oil.
3. Using a pastry brush, apply the marinade to the roast, coating all surfaces. Cover it with plastic wrap and allow it to sit until the meat comes to room temperature, about 1 hour.
4. When ready to cook, set grill temperature to High and preheat, lid closed for 15 minutes.
5. Arrange the roasting pan with the pork on the grill grate. Roast for 30 minute.
6. Reduce the heat to 325°F (163°C). Loosely fill the crown with the stuffing, mounding it at the top. Cover the stuffing with foil. (Alternatively, you can bake the stuffing in a separate pan alongside the roast.)
7. Roast the pork for another 1-½ hours. Remove the foil from the stuffing and continue to roast until the internal temperature of the meat is 150°F (66°C), about 30 minute to an hour. Make sure the temperature probe doesn't touch bone or you will get a false reading.

8. Remove roast from grill and allow to rest for 15 minutes. Remove the foil covering the bones, but leave the butcher's string on the roast until ready to carve. Transfer to a warm platter.

Stuffed Pork Loin with Bacon

Prep time: 20 minutes | Cook time: 1 hour | Serves 4 to 6

- 3 pound (1.4 kg) pork loin, butterflied
- As needed pork rub
- ¼ cup Walnuts, chopped
- ⅓ cup Craisins
- 1 tablespoon oregano, fresh
- 1 tablespoon fresh thyme
- 6 pieces Asparagus, fresh
- 6 slices Bacon, sliced
- 1/3 cup Parmesan cheese, grated
- As needed bacon grease

1. Lay down 2 large pieces of butcher's twine on your work surface. Place butterflied pork loin perpendicular to twine.
2. Season the inside of the pork loin with the pork rub.
3. On one end of the loin, layer in a line all of the ingredients, beginning with the chopped walnuts, craisins, oregano, thyme, and asparagus.
4. Add bacon and top with the parmesan cheese.
5. Starting at the end with all of the fillings, carefully roll up the pork loin and secure on both ends with butcher's twine.
6. Roll the pork loin in the reserved bacon grease and season the outside with more Pork Rub.
7. When ready to cook, set temperature to 180°F (82°C) and preheat, lid closed for 15 minutes. Place stuffed pork loin directly on the grill grate and smoke for 1 hour.
8. Remove the pork loin; increase the temperature to 350°F (177°C) and allow to preheat.
9. Place the loin back on the Traeger and grill for approximately 30 to 45 minutes or until the temperature reads 135°F (57°C) on an instant-read thermometer.
10. Move the pork loin to a plate and tent it with aluminum foil. Let it rest for 15 minutes before slicing and serving. Enjoy!

Porchetta with Italian Salsa Verde

Prep time: 30 minutes | Cook time: 3 hours | Serves 8 to 12

- 3 tablespoon dried fennel seed
- 2 tablespoon red pepper flakes
- 2 tablespoon sage, minced
- 1 tablespoon rosemary, minced
- 3 clove garlic, minced
- As needed lemon zest
- As needed orange zest
- Salt and pepper, to taste
- 6 pound (2.7 kg) pork belly, skin on
- 1 whole shallot, thinly sliced
- 6 tablespoon parsley, minced
- 2 tablespoon freshly minced chives
- 1 tablespoon oregano, fresh
- 3 tablespoon white wine vinegar
- ½ teaspoon kosher salt
- ¾ cup olive oil
- ½ teaspoon Dijon mustard
- As needed fresh lemon juice

1. Prepare herb mixture: In a medium bowl, mix together fennel seeds, red pepper flakes, sage, rosemary, garlic, citrus zest, salt and pepper.
2. Place pork belly skin side up on a clean work surface and score in a crosshatch pattern. Flip the pork belly over and season flesh side with salt, pepper and half of the herb mixture.
3. Place trimmed pork loin in the center of the belly and rub with remaining herb mixture. Season with salt and pepper.
4. Roll the pork belly around the loin to form a cylindrical shape and tie tightly with kitchen twine at 1" intervals.
5. Season the outside with salt and pepper and transfer to refrigerator, uncovered and let air dry overnight.
6. When ready to cook, start the Traeger grill and set to smoke.
7. Fit a rimmed baking sheet with a rack and place the pork on the rack seam side down.

8. Place the pan directly on the grill grate and smoke for 1 hour.

9. Increase the grill temperature to 325°F (163°C) and roast until the internal temperature of the meat reaches 135°F (57°C), about 2½ hours. If the exterior begins to burn before the desired internal temperature is reached, tent with foil.

10. Remove from grill and let stand 30 minute before slicing.

11. To make the Italian salsa verde: Combine shallot, parsley, chives, vinegar, oregano and salt in a medium bowl. Whisk in olive oil then stir in mustard and lemon juice.

12. Drizzle slices with Italian salsa verde and enjoy!

BBQ St. Louis-Style Ribs

Prep time: 5 minutes | Cook time: 6 hours 10 minutes | Serves 4

- 2 racks of St. Louis-style ribs
- ¼ cup Traeger Pork & Poultry Rub
- 1 cup apple juice
- 1 bottle Traeger Sweet & Heat BBQ Sauce

1. Trim the ribs and peel off the membrane from the back of the ribs. Brush the Traeger Pork & Poultry Rub all over the ribs. Let marinate for 20 minutes and up to 4 hours if refrigerated.
2. When ready to cook, set wood pellet grill temperature to 225°F (107°C) and preheat, lid closed for 15 minutes.
3. Place the ribs, bone-side down, on the grill grate. Pour the apple juice in a spray bottle and spritz the ribs evenly. Smoke for 3 hours.
4. Remove the ribs from the grill and wrap in aluminum foil. Leave an opening at one end, pour in the remaining apple juice into the foil and wrap tightly.
5. Place the ribs back on the grill, meat-side down. Smoke for an additional 3 hours.
6. After 1 hour, start checking the internal temperature of the ribs. The ribs are done when the internal temperature reaches 203°F (95°C).
7. When done, remove from the foil and brush the Traeger Sweet & Heat BBQ Sauce all over the ribs.
8. Return to the grill and cook for an additional 10 minutes to set the sauce.
9. After sauce has set, take the ribs off the grill and let rest for 10 minutes.
10. Slice the ribs in between the bones and serve warm.

GRILLED VEGETABLE RECIPES

Roasted Parmesan Cheese Broccoli

Preparation Time: 5 min | Cooking Time: 45 min | Servings: 3 to 4

- 3 cups broccoli, stems trimmed
- 1 tbsp lemon juice
- 1 tbsp olive oil
- 2 garlic cloves, minced
- 1/2 tsp kosher salt
- 1/2 tsp ground black pepper
- 1 tsp lemon zest
- 1/8 cup parmesan cheese, grated

Preheat pellet grill to 375°F.

Place broccoli in a resealable bag. Add lemon juice, olive oil, garlic cloves, salt, and pepper. Seal the bag and toss to combine. Let the mixture marinate for 30 minutes.

Pour broccoli into a grill basket. Place the basket on grill grates to roast. Grill broccoli for 14-18 minutes, flipping broccoli halfway through. Grill until tender yet a little crispy on the outside.

Remove broccoli from the grill and place on a serving dish — zest with lemon and top with grated parmesan cheese. Serve immediately and enjoy!

Bacon-Wrapped Jalapeno Poppers

Preparation Time: 15 min | Cooking Time: 40 min | Servings: 8 to 12

- 12 large jalapeño peppers
- 8 oz cream cheese, softened
- 1 cup pepper jack cheese, shredded
- Juice of 1 lemon 1/2 tsp garlic powder
- 1/4 tsp kosher salt
- 1/4 tsp ground black pepper
- 12 bacon slices, cut in half

Preheat pellet grill to 400°F.
Slice jalapeños in half lengthwise. Remove seeds and scrape sides with a spoon to remove the membrane.
In a medium bowl, mix cream cheese, pepper jack cheese, garlic powder, salt, and pepper until thoroughly combined.
Use a spoon or knife to place the cream cheese mixture into each jalapeño half. Make sure not to fill over the sides of the jalapeño half. Wrap each cheese-filled pepper with a half slice of bacon. If you can't get a secure wrap, then hold bacon and pepper together with a toothpick.
Place assembled poppers on the grill and cook for 15-20 minutes or until bacon is crispy.
Remove from the grill, allow to cool, then serve and enjoy!

Kale Chips

Preparation time: 10 minutes | Cooking time: 20 minutes | Servings: 6

- 2 bunches of kale, stems removed
- ½ teaspoon of sea salt
- 4 tablespoons olive oil

Switch on the Traeger grill, fill the grill hopper with apple-flavored wood pellets, power the grill on by using the control panel, select 'smoke' on the temperature dial, or set the temperature to 250 degrees F and let it preheat for a minimum of 15 minutes.

Meanwhile, rinse the kale leaves, pat dry, spread the kale on a sheet tray, drizzle with oil, season with salt and toss until well coated. When the grill has preheated, open the lid, place sheet tray on the grill grate, shut the grill, and smoke for 20 minutes until crisp.
Serve straight away.

Grilled Zucchini

Preparation time: 5 minutes | Cooking time: 10 minutes | Servings: 6

- 4 medium zucchinis
- 2 tablespoons olive oil
- 1 tablespoon sherry vinegar
- 2 sprigs of thyme, leaves chopped
- ½ teaspoon salt
- 1/3 teaspoon ground black pepper

Switch on the wood pellet grill grill, fill the grill hopper with oak flavored wood pellets, power the grill on by using the control panel, select 'smoke' on the temperature dial, or set the temperature to 350 degrees F and let it preheat for a minimum of 5 minutes. Meanwhile, cut the ends of each zucchini, cut each in half and then into thirds, and place in a plastic bag.

Add remaining ingredients, seal the bag, and shake well to coat zucchini pieces. When the grill has preheated, open the lid, place zucchini on the grill grate, shut the grill, and smoke for 4 minutes per side. When done, transfer zucchini to a dish, garnish with more thyme and then serve.

Vegetable Sandwich

Preparation time: 30 minutes | Cooking time: 45 minutes | Servings: 4

For the Smoked Hummus:
- 1 1/2 cups cooked chickpeas
- 1 tablespoon minced garlic
- 1 teaspoon salt
- 4 tablespoons lemon juice
- 2 tablespoon olive oil
- 1/3 cup tahini

For the Vegetables:
- 2 large portobello mushrooms
- 1 small eggplant, destemmed, sliced into strips
- 1 teaspoon salt
- 1 small zucchini, trimmed, sliced into strips
- ½ teaspoon ground black pepper
- 1 small yellow squash, peeled, sliced into strips
- ¼ cup olive oil

For the Cheese:
- 1 lemon, juiced
- ½ teaspoon minced garlic
- ¼ teaspoon ground black pepper
- ¼ teaspoon salt
- 1/2 cup ricotta cheese To Assemble:
- 1 bunch basil, leaves chopped
- 2 heirloom tomatoes, sliced
- 4 ciabatta buns, halved

Switch on the wood pellet grill, fill the grill hopper with pecan flavored wood pellets, power the grill on by using the control panel, select 'smoke' on the temperature dial, or set the temperature to 180 degrees F and let it preheat for a minimum of 15 minutes.

Meanwhile, prepare the hummus, and for this, take a sheet tray and spread chickpeas on it.

When the grill has preheated, open the lid, place sheet tray on the grill grate, shut the grill, and smoke for 20 minutes.

When done, transfer chickpeas to a food processor, add remaining ingredients for the hummus in it and pulse for 2 minutes until smooth, set aside until req uired.

Change the smoking temperature to 500 degrees F, shut with lid, and let it preheat for 10 minutes.

Meanwhile, prepare vegetables and for this, take a large bowl, place all the vegetables in it, add salt and black pepper, drizzle with oil and lemon juice and toss until coated.

Place vegetables on the grill grate, shut with lid, then smoke for eggplant, zucchini, and squash for 15 minutes and mushrooms for 25 minutes.

Meanwhile, prepare the cheese and for this, take a small bowl, place all of its ingredients in it and stir until well combined. Assemble the sandwich for this, cut buns in half lengthwise, spread prepared hummus on one side, spread cheese on the other side, then stuff with grilled vegetables and top with tomatoes and basil. Serve straight away.

Grilled Potato Salad

Preparation time: 15 minutes | Cooking time: 10 minutes | Servings: 8

- 1 ½ pound fingerling potatoes, halved lengthwise
- 1 small jalapeno, sliced
- 10 scallions
- 2 teaspoons salt
- 2 tablespoons rice vinegar
- 2 teaspoons lemon juice 2/3 cup olive oil, divided

Switch on the wood pellet grill, fill the grill hopper with pecan flavored wood pellets, power the grill on by using the control panel, select 'smoke' on the temperature dial, or set the temperature to 450 degrees F and let it preheat for a minimum of 5 minutes.

Meanwhile, prepare scallions, and for this, brush them with some oil. When the grill has preheated, open the lid, place scallions on the grill grate, shut the grill, and smoke for 3 minutes until lightly charred. Then transfer scallions to a cutting board, let them cool for 5 minutes, then cut into slices and set aside until req uired. Brush potatoes with some oil, season with some salt and black pepper, place potatoes on the grill grate, shut the grill, and smoke for 5 minutes until thoroughly cooked. Then take a large bowl, pour in remaining oil, add salt, lemon juice, and vinegar and stir until combined. Add grilled scallion and potatoes, toss until well mixed, taste to adjust seasoning, and then serve.

Green Beans with Bacon

Preparation time: 10 minutes | Cooking time: 20 minutes | Servings: 6

- 4 strips of bacon, chopped
- 1 1/2-pound green beans, ends trimmed
- 1 teaspoon minced garlic
- 1 teaspoon salt 4 tablespoons olive oil

Switch on the wood pellet grill, fill the grill hopper with flavored wood pellets, power the grill on by using the control panel, select 'smoke' on the temperature dial, or set the temperature to 450 degrees F and let it preheat for a minimum of 15 minutes.

Meanwhile, take a sheet tray, place all the ingredients in it and toss until mixed. When the grill has preheated, open the lid, place the prepared sheet tray on the grill grate, shut the grill, and smoke for 20 minutes until lightly browned and cooked. When done, transfer green beans to a dish and then serve.

Grilled Eggplants

Preparation Time: 5 minutes | Cooking Time: 12 minutes | Servings: 6

- 1 to 2 large eggplants
- 3 tablespoons of extra virgin olive oil
- 2 tablespoons of balsamic vinegar
- 2 finely minced garlic cloves
- 1 pinch of each thyme, dill; oregano, and basil

1. Gather your ingredients.
2. Heat your wood pellet grill grill to a medium-high
3. When the Traeger grill becomes hot; slice the eggplant into slices of about 1/2-inch of thickness
4. In a bowl, whisk all together with the olive oil with the balsamic vinegar, the garlic, the herbs, the salt, and the pepper.
5. Brush both sides of the sliced eggplant
with oil and with the vinegar mixture.
6. Place the eggplant over the preheated
    grill
7. Grill the eggplant for about 12 minutes
    Serve and enjoy!

Grilled Asparagus

Prep Time:5 Minutes | Cook Time: 20 Minutes | Servings: 4

- 3 cups of vegetables sliced
- 2 tbsp of olive oil
- 2 tbsp of garlic & herb seasoning

Preheat your wood pellet grill grill to a temperature of about 350°F While your Traeger is heating, slice the vegetables.

Cut the spears from the Broccoli and the Zucchini; then wash the outsides and slice into spears, Cut the peppers into wide strips. You can also grill carrots, corn, asparagus, and potatoes. Grill at a temperature of about 350°F for about 20 minutes. Serve and enjoy!

1. Bron Johnson

THE
WOOD PELLET
SMOKER & GRILL
COOKBOOK

COOKBOOK 2
LUSCIOUS BBQ LAMB RECIPES

- THE -
EST. **OLD** 1999
TEXAS
PITMASTER
- TRAVIS COUNTY -

Lamb Kabobs

Preparation Time: 8 minutes | Cooking Time: 35 minutes | Servings:6

- 1 ¼ cup of olive oil
- 1 ¼ cup of sherry
- 1 or 2 red onions, medium
- 1 Heaped tablespoon of GMG Wild Game Rub
- 1 Heaped tablespoon of ground black pepper
- 5 Garlic cloves
- A leg of lamb

Trim the fat from the lamb; then cut the lamb into cubes of about 1 ½ inch
Place in a large bowl; then sprinkle the rub over the meat and toss until your ingredients are very well combined
If you don't have an already prepared rub; just combine 1 teaspoon of brown sugar with 1 teaspoon of salt, ¼ teaspoon of turmeric; and ¼ teaspoon of ginger.

Peel the garlic and press to mash it
Chop the onion into rough dices in a small bowl; then chop a few sprigs of parsley
Add the liquid to the onion; then; mix and pour the mixture of the onion over the cubed lamb and place in the refrigerator for an overnight
Skewer the lamb chunks into wooden skewers
Grill the kabobs at a temperature of about 360-380° for about 25 to 35 minutes
Remove the meat from the grill Serve and enjoy your dish!

Grilled Lamb liver

Preparation Time: 5 minutes | Cooking Time: 15 minutes | Servings: 3

- 1 lb. of lamb liver; chopped into thin slices
- ½ Cup of olive oil
- 1 Crushed garlic clove
- 1 tbsp of fresh finely chopped mint
- 1 tsp of salt
- ¼ tsp of black pepper freshly ground

Preheat the wood pellet grill over medium-high heat.
Rinse the lamb liver thoroughly under cold running water.
Pat the liver dry with a clean paper towel; then using a sharp knife; remove the tough veins; then cut into thin slices In a small bowl, combine the olive oil with the crushed garlic, the mint, the salt, and the pepper.

Mix very well until your ingredients are very well incorporated Generously brush the slices of the liver with the mixture and grill for about 5 to 7 minutes on each of the sides.
Remove from the heat; then serve and enjoy!

Leg of Lamb

Preparation Time: 10 minutes | Cooking Time: 2 hours | Servings: 6

- 2 teaspoons extra virgin olive oil
- 1 tablespoon crushed garlic
- 7 pounds bone-in leg of lamb
- 4 cloves of garlic, sliced lengthwise
- 4 sprig rosemary, cut into 1-inch pieces
- 2 lemons, sliced Salt and pepper to taste

Combine olive oil and crushed garlic. Rub the mixture on the leg of the lamb. Make small perforations in the lamb using a sharp knife and stuff the slivered garlic and rosemary sprigs. Zest and juice the lemons and sprinkle over the lamb. Season with salt and pepper to taste. When ready to cook, fire the Traeger Grill to 5000F.

Use desired wood pellets when cooking. Close the lid and preheat for 15 minutes. Place the seasoned leg of lamb on the grill grate and reduce the grill to 3500F. Cook for 2 hours. Let the lamb rest for 15 minutes before carving.

Grilled Lamb

Preparation Time: 10 minutes | Cooking Time: 16 minutes | Servings: 6

- ½ cup olive oil
- ½ tablespoon salt
- 2 teaspoons black pepper
- 2 tablespoons chopped mint
- ½ tablespoon cilantro, chopped
- 1 teaspoon cumin
- ½ cup lemon juice
- 3 pounds boneless leg of lamb, cut into 2-inch cubes
- 15 apricots, halved and seeded
- 5 onions, cut into wedges

In a bowl, combine the oil, salt, pepper, mint, cilantro, cumin, and lemon juice.

Massage the mixture onto the lamb shoulder and allow it to marinate in the fridge for at least 2 hours.

Remove the lamb from the marinade and thread the lamb, apricots, and red onion alternatingly on a skewer.

When ready to cook, fire the Traeger Grill to 4000F. Use desired wood pellets when cooking. Close the lid and preheat for 15 minutes.

Place the skewers on the grill grate and cook for 8 minutes on each side.

Remove from the grill.

Braised Lamb Shank

Preparation Time: 10 minutes | Cooking Time: 4 hours | Servings: 6

- 6 whole lamb shanks
- Traeger Prime Rib Rub
- 1 cup beef broth
- 1 cup red wine
- 4 sprig rosemary and thyme

Season the lamb shanks with Traeger Prime Rib Rub.
When ready to cook, fire the wood pellet grill to 5000F. Use desired wood pellets when cooking. Close the lid and preheat for 15 minutes. Place the lamb shanks directly on the grill grate and cook for 20 minutes or until the surface browns.

Transfer the shanks to a Dutch oven and pour in beef broth.
Place the Dutch oven back on the grill grate and reduce the temperature to 3250F. Cook for another 3 to 4 hours.

Smoked Lamb Leg with Salsa Verde

Preparation Time: 10 minutes | Cooking Time: 3 hours | Servings: 6

- 2 tablespoons oil
- 1 whole leg of lamb, fat trimmed and cut into chunks
- Salt to taste
- 6 cloves green garlic, unpeeled
- 1-pound tomatillos, husked and washed
- 1 small yellow onion, quartered
- 5 whole serrano chili peppers
- 1 tablespoon capers, drained
- ¼ cup cilantro, finely chopped
- ½ teaspoon sugar
- 1 cup chicken broth
- 3 tablespoons lime juice, freshly squeezed

Fire the wood pellet grill to 5000F. Use desired wood pellets when cooking. Close the lid and preheat for 15 minutes.
Place a Dutch oven on the grill grate and add oil.
Put the lamb in the Dutch oven and season with salt to taste. Stir once then close the lid.

Place the garlic, tomatillos, onion, serrano peppers, and capers in a parchment-lined baking tray.
Season with salt to taste and drizzle with olive oil.
Place in the grill and cook for 15 minutes.
Remove the vegetables from the grill and transfer to a blender. Add cilantro and sugar.

Season with more salt if needed. Pulse until smooth then set aside.
Pour the mixture into the Dutch oven and add in chicken broth and lime juice. Cook for 3 hours.

Grilled Lamb Chops with Rosemary

Preparation Time: 10 minutes | Cooking Time: 12 minutes | Servings:4

- ½ cup extra virgin olive oil
- ¼ cup coarsely chopped onion
- 2 cloves of garlic, minced
- 2 tablespoons soy sauce
- 2 tablespoons balsamic vinegar
- 1 tablespoon fresh rosemary
- 2 teaspoons Dijon mustard
- 1 teaspoon Worcestershire sauce
- Salt and pepper to taste 4 lamb chops (8 ounces each)

Heat oil in a saucepan over medium flame and sauté the onion and garlic until fragrant. Place in a food processor together with the soy sauce, vinegar, rosemary, mustard, Worcestershire sauce, salt, and pepper. Pulse until smooth. Set aside.

Fire the wood pellet grill to 5000F. Use desired wood pellets when cooking. Close the lid and preheat for 15 minutes. Brush the lamb chops on both sides with the paste. Place on the grill grates and cook for 6 minutes per side or until the internal temperature reaches 1350F for medium-rare. Serve with the paste if you have leftovers.

Rack of Lamb

Preparation Time: 20 minutes | Cooking Time: 75 minutes | Servings:4

- 1/2 cup olive oil
- ½ cup dry mustard
- ¼ cup hot chili powder
- 2 tablespoons freshly squeezed lemon juice
- 2 tablespoon onion, minced
- 1 tablespoon paprika
- 1 tablespoon dried thyme
- 1 tablespoon salt
- 1 American rack of lamb, 7-9 chops
- Mint Sauce
- ¼ cup fresh mint leaves, chopped ¼ cup hot water
- 2 tablespoons apple cider vinegar
- 2 tablespoons brown sugar
- ½ teaspoon salt
- ½ teaspoon fresh ground pepper

Take a small bowl and mix in olive oil, mustard, chili powder, lemon juice, onion, paprika, thyme, Worcestershire sauce, salt
Preheat your smoker to 200 degrees F

Rub the paste all over the lamb and transfer to the smoker, smoke for 75 minutes until internal temperature reaches 145 degrees F
Remove lamb from heat and let it rest for a few minutes, serve with mint sauce Enjoy!

Mouthwatering Lamb Chops

Preparation Time: 15 minutes | Cooking Time: 20 minutes | Servings: 4

- For Marinade
- ½ cup of rice wine vinegar
- 1 teaspoon liquid smoke
- 2 tablespoons extra virgin olive oil
- 2 tablespoons dried onion, minced
- 1 tablespoon fresh mint, chopped
- Lamb Chops
- 8 (4 ounces0 lamb chops
- ½ cup hot pepper jelly
- 1 tablespoon Sriracha
- 1 teaspoon salt
- 1 teaspoon freshly ground black pepper

Take a small bowl and whisk in rice wine vinegar, liquid smoke, olive oil, minced onion, and mint

Add lamb chops in an aluminum roasting pan, pour marinade over meat and turn well to coat

Cover with plastic wrap and marinate for 2 hours

Preheat your smoker to 165 degrees F

Take a small saucepan and place it over low heat, add hot pepper jelly and sriracha, keep it warm

Once ready to cook chops, remove them from marinade and pat dry Discard marinade

Season chops with salt, pepper, and transfer to the grill grate

Close and smoke for 5 minutes

Remove chops from grill and increase the temperature to 450°F.

Transfer chops to grill and sear for 2 minutes per side until the internal temperature reaches 145 degrees F Serve chops and enjoy!

Greek Lamb Leg

Preparation Time:15 minutes | CookingTime:25 minutes | Servings:12

- 2 tablespoons fresh rosemary, chopped
- 1 tablespoon ground thyme
- 5 garlic cloves, minced
- 2 tablespoons salt
- 1 tablespoon fresh ground pepper
- Butcher's string
- 1 whole boneless (6-8 pounds) leg of lamb
- ¼ cup extra virgin olive oil
- 1 cup red wine vinegar
- ½ cup canola oil

Take a small bowl and add rosemary, thyme, garlic, salt, pepper and keep it on the side
Use butcher's string and tie leg of lamb in the shape of the roast
Rub lamb generously with olive oil mix and spice mix
Transfer to plate and cover with plastic wrap
Chill for 4 hours.

Remove lamb from the fridge
Preheat your Smoker to 325 degrees F
Take a small bowl and add red wine vinegar and canola oil
Place lamb directly on the grill and close lid, smoke for 20-25 minutes per pound, making sure to keep basing after every 30 minutes
Once the thickest part reaches 145 degrees F, the lamb is ready
Let it rest for a while and serve Enjoy!

Moroccan Lamb Ribs

Preparation Time: 15 minutes | Cooking Time: 3 hours | Servings: 12

- 2 racks lamb, membrane removed
- Rub
- 2 tablespoons paprika
- ½ tablespoon coriander seeds
- ½ tablespoon salt
- 1 teaspoon cumin seeds
- 1 teaspoon ground allspice
- 1 teaspoon powdered lemon peel
- ½ teaspoon ground black pepper

Preheat your smoker to 250 degrees F
Take a bowl and mix in paprika, coriander seeds, salt, cumin seeds, ground allspice, lemon peel, pepper, and using a mortar and pestle to grind.

Season both sides of lamb
Transfer to your smoker and smoke for 3 hours until tender
Remove from smoker and serve
Enjoy!

Christmas Garlicky Lamb

Prep time: 1 hour | Cook time: 1 to 2 hours | Serves 4

- 2 racks of lamb, trimmed, frenched, and tied into a crown
- 1¼ cups extra-virgin olive oil, divided 2 tablespoons chopped fresh basil
- 2 tablespoons chopped fresh rosemary
- 2 tablespoons ground sage
- 2 tablespoons ground thyme
- 8 garlic cloves, minced
- 2 teaspoons salt
- 2 teaspoons freshly ground black pepper

1. Set the lamb out on the counter to take the chill off, about an hour.
2. In a small bowl, combine 1 cup of olive oil, the basil, rosemary, sage, thyme, garlic, salt, and pepper.
3. Baste the entire crown with the herbed olive oil and wrap the exposed frenched bones in aluminum foil.
4. Supply your smoker with wood pellets and follow the manufacturer's specific start-up procedure. Preheat, with the lid closed, to 275°F (135°C).
5. Put the lamb directly on the grill, close the lid, and smoke for 1 hour 30 minute to 2 hours, or until a meat thermometer inserted in the thickest part reads 140°F (60°C).
6. Remove the lamb from the heat, tent with foil, and let rest for about 15 minutes before serving. The temperature will rise about 5°F (-15°C) during the rest period, for a finished temperature of 145°F (63°C).

Lamb with Pitas

Prep time: 20 minutes | Cook time: 40 minutes | Serves 4

- 1 pound (454 g) ground lamb
- 2 teaspoons salt
- 1 teaspoon freshly ground black pepper
- 2 tablespoons chopped fresh oregano
- 1 tablespoon minced garlic
- 1 tablespoon onion powder
- 4 to 6 pocketless pitas
- Tzatziki sauce, for serving
- 1 tomato, chopped, for serving
- 1 small onion, thinly sliced, for serving

1. In a medium bowl, combine the lamb, salt, pepper, oregano, garlic, and onion powder; mix well. Cover with plastic wrap and refrigerate overnight.
2. Supply your smoker with wood pellets and follow the manufacturer's specific start-up procedure. Preheat, with the lid closed, to 300°F (149°C).
3. Remove the meat mixture from the refrigerator and, on a Frogmat or a piece of heavy-duty aluminum foil, roll and shape it into a rectangular loaf about 8 inches long by 5 inches wide.
4. Place the loaf directly on the grill, close the lid, and smoke for 35 minutes, or until a meat thermometer inserted in the center reads 155°F (68°C).
5. Remove the loaf from the heat and increase the temperature to 450°F (232°C).
6. Cut the loaf into ⅛-inch slices and place on a Frogmat or a piece of heavy-duty foil.

7. Return the meat (still on the Frogmat or foil) to the smoker, close the lid, and continue cooking for 2 to 4 minutes, or until the edges are crispy.

8. Warm the pitas in the smoker for a few minutes and serve with the lamb, tzatziki sauce, chopped tomato, and sliced onion.

Rosemary Lamb Chops

Prep time: 15 minutes | Cook time: 2 hours | Serves 4

- 4½ pounds (2 kg) bone-in lamb chops
- 2 tablespoons olive oil
- Salt, to taste
- Freshly ground black pepper, to taste
- 1 bunch fresh rosemary

1. Supply your smoker with wood pellets and follow the manufacturer's specific start-up procedure. Preheat the grill, with the lid closed, to 180°F (82°C).
2. Rub the lamb chops all over with olive oil and season on both sides with salt and pepper.
3. Spread the rosemary directly on the grill grate, creating a surface area large enough for all the chops to rest on. Place the chops on the rosemary and smoke until they reach an internal temperature of 135°F (57°C).
4. Increase the grill's temperature to 450°F (232°C), remove the rosemary, and continue to cook the chops until their internal temperature reaches 145°F (63°C).
5. Remove the chops from the grill and let them rest for 5 minutes before serving.

Rosemary-Garlic Rack of Lamb

Prep time: 25 minutes | Cook time: 4 to 6 hours | Serves 6

- 1 (2-pound / 907-g) rack of lamb
- 1 batch Rosemary-Garlic Lamb Seasoning

1. Supply your smoker with wood pellets and follow the manufacturer's specific start-up procedure. Preheat the grill, with the lid closed, to 225°F (107°C).
2. Using a boning knife, score the bottom fat portion of the rib meat.
3. Using your hands, rub the rack of lamb all over with the seasoning, making sure it penetrates into the scored fat.
4. Place the rack directly on the grill grate, fat-side up, and smoke until its internal temperature reaches 145°F (63°C).
5. Remove the rack from the grill and let it rest for 20 to 30 minute, before slicing it into individual ribs to serve.

Grilled Lamb and Apricot Kabobs

Prep time: 15 minutes | Cook time: 8 to 10 minutes | Serves 4

- ½ cup olive oil
- ½ cup lemon juice
- 2 tablespoons minced fresh mint
- 1 tablespoon lemon zest
- ½ tablespoon finely chopped cilantro
- ½ tablespoon salt
- 2 teaspoons black pepper
- 1 teaspoon cumin
- 3 pounds (1.4 kg) boneless leg of lamb, cut into 2-inch cubes
- 15 whole dried apricots
- 2 whole red onions, cut into ⅛-inch thick

1. In a medium bowl, stir together the olive oil, lemon juice, mint, lemon zest, cilantro, salt, pepper and cumin. Add the lamb shoulder to the bowl and toss to coat. Set in the refrigerator and marinate overnight.
2. Remove the lamb from the marinade and thread lamb, apricots, and red onion alternatively until the skewer is full.
3. When ready to cook, set Traeger temperature to 400°F (204°C) and preheat, lid closed for 15 minutes.
4. Lay the skewers on the grill grate and cook for 8 to 10 minutes, or until the onions are lightly browned and the lamb is cooked to the desired temperature.
5. Remove the skewers from the grill and serve immediately.

Spicy Braised Lamb Shoulder

Prep time: 10 minutes | Cook time: 5 hours 2 minutes | Serves 4

- 2 ounces (57 g) guajillo peppers, deseeded
- 2 tablespoons plus ½ cup water, divided
- 3 cloves garlic
- 2 tablespoons olive oil
- 1 tablespoon lime juice
- 1 tablespoon smoked paprika
- 1 tablespoon fresh oregano
- 1 tablespoon salt
- ¼ tablespoon ground coriander seeds
- ¼ tablespoon ground cumin seeds
- ¼ tablespoon ground pumpkin seeds
- 3 pounds (1.4 kg) lamb shoulders

1. In a microwave-safe bowl, cover the guajillo chilies with water and microwave on high for 2 minutes. Let cool slightly, then transfer the soft chilies and 2 tablespoons of the water to a blender.
2. Add the remaining ingredients, except for the lamb shoulders, to the blender. Pulse until smooth.
3. Arrange the lamb in a roast pan and rub ½ cup of the sauce all over the meat. Let marinate at room temperature for at least 2 hours and up to 12 hours.
4. When ready to cook, set wood pellet grill temperature to 325°F (163°C) and preheat, lid closed for 15 minutes.
5. Add ½ cup of the water to the roast pan and cover the pan loosely with foil. Cook the lamb for 2½ hours, adding water to the pan a few times.
6. Remove the foil and cook for another 2½ hours, or until the lamb is browned and tender, occasionally spooning the juices on top.

7. Remove from the grill and let cool for 20 minutes before shredding. Spoon the remaining liquid in the bottom of the pan over the lamb.
8. Serve immediately.

Grilled Lamb Leg

Prep time: 10 minutes | Cook time: 30 to 40 minutes | Serves 8

- 5 pounds (2.3 kg) leg of lamb, butterflied and boneless
- 1 whole onion, sliced into rings Marinade:
- 1 whole lemon, juiced and rinds reserved
- 4 cloves garlic, minced
- 1 cup olive oil
- ¼ cup red wine vinegar
- 2½ teaspoons minced rosemary
- 1 teaspoon thyme
- 1 teaspoon salt
- 1 teaspoon ground black pepper

1. In a mixing bowl, whisk together all the ingredients for the marinade.
2. Remove any netting from the lamb and place into a large resealable plastic bag. Pour the marinade into the bag and add the onion. Massage the bag to distribute the marinade and herbs. Refrigerate for several hours or overnight.
3. Remove the lamb from the marinade and pat dry with paper towels. Discard the marinade.
4. When ready to cook, set the wood pellet grill to High and preheat, lid closed for 15 minutes.
5. Arrange the lamb on the grill grate, fat-side down. Grill for 30 to 40 minutes per side, or until the internal temperature reaches 135°F (57°C) for medium-rare.
6. Let the lamb leg cool for 5 minutes before slicing. Serve warm.

Roasted Breaded Rack of Lamb

Prep time: 10 minutes | Cook time: 20 minutes | Serves 4

- 1 rack of lamb, frenched (about 1½ pounds / 680 g)
- ½ cup yellow mustard
- 1 tablespoon salt
- 1 teaspoon ground black pepper
- 1 cup panko bread crumbs
- 1 tablespoon minced Italian parsley
- 1 teaspoon minced rosemary
- 1 teaspoon minced sage

1. Rub the rack of lamb with the mustard and season with salt and pepper.
2. In a shallow baking dish, combine the remaining ingredients. Dredge the lamb in the bread crumb mixture.
3. When ready to cook, set wood pellet grill temperature to 500°F (260°C) and preheat, lid closed for 15 minutes.
4. Place the rack of lamb on the grill grate, bone-side down, and cook for 20 minutes, or until the internal temperature reaches 120°F (49°C).
5. Remove from the grill and let rest for 5 to 10 minutes before slicing. Serve warm.

Garlicky Grilled Rack of Lamb

Prep time: 5 minutes | Cook time: 30 minutes | Serves 4

- 8 cloves garlic
- 1 bunch fresh thyme
- 1 tablespoon kosher salt
- 2 teaspoons extra-virgin olive oil
- 1 teaspoon sherry vinegar
- 2 pounds (907 g) rack of lamb

1. In a blender, combine all the ingredients, except for the rack of lamb. Pulse until smooth. Rub the paste all over the rack of lamb.
2. When ready to cook, set wood pellet grill temperature to 450°F (232°C) and preheat, lid closed for 15 minutes.
3. Lay the rack of lamb, fat-side down, on the grill and cook for 20 minutes. Turn over so the fat side is up and cook for an additional 10 minutes. A thermometer inserted in the center of the lamb should register 160°F (71°C).
4. Let cool for 10 minutes before slicing into chops. Serve warm.

INCREDIBLE BBQ VEGETABLE RECIPES

Balsamic Mexican Street Corn

Prep time: 15 minutes | Cook time: 45 minutes | Serves 6

- 16 to 20 long toothpicks
- 1 pound (454 g) Brussels sprouts, trimmed and wilted, leaves removed
- ½ pound (227 g) bacon, cut in half
- 1 tablespoon packed brown sugar
- 1 tablespoon Cajun seasoning
- ¼ cup balsamic vinegar
- ¼ cup extra-virgin olive oil
- ¼ cup chopped fresh cilantro
- 2 teaspoons minced garlic

1. Soak the toothpicks in water for 15 minutes.
2. Supply your smoker with wood pellets and follow the manufacturer's specific start-up procedure. Preheat, with the lid closed, to 300°F (149°C).
3. Wrap each Brussels sprout in a half slice of bacon and secure with a toothpick.
4. In a small bowl, combine the brown sugar and Cajun seasoning. Dip each wrapped Brussels sprout in this sweet rub and roll around to coat.
5. Place, the sprouts on a Frogman or parchment paper-lined baking sheet on the grill grate, close the lid, and smoke for 45 minutes to 1 hour, turning as needed, until cooked evenly and the bacon is crisp.
6. In a small bowl, whisk together the balsamic vinegar, olive oil, cilantro, and garlic.
7. Remove the toothpicks from the Brussels sprouts, transfer to a plate and serve drizzled with the cilantrobalsamic sauce.

Potato Fries with Chipotle Ketchup

Prep time: 10 minutes | Cook time: 10 to 15 minutes | Serves 4

Chipotle Ketchup:

- 4 whole chipotle peppers, chopped
- 1 cup ketchup
- 1 tablespoon extra-virgin olive oil
- 1 teaspoon garlic powder 1 teaspoon onion powder
- 1 tablespoon chili powder
- 1 tablespoon sugar
- 1 tablespoon cumin
- 1 whole limes Fries:
- 6 whole Yukon gold potatoes, cut into thick strips
- 2 tablespoons butter, melted
- 1 tablespoon Traeger Beef Rub
- ¼ cup chopped flat-leaf parsley

1. Stir together all the chipotle ketchup in a mixing bowl until combined. Place in the refrigerator for at least 1 hour to blend the flavors (making it one day ahead of time is even better if you can swing it).
2. When ready to cook, set wood pellet grill temperature to High and preheat, lid closed for 15 minutes.
3. Place the potatoes in a bowl, drizzle with melted butter and sprinkle with the Beef rub, tossing to coat.
4. Lay the potatoes on a Traeger Grilling Basket and bake for 10 to 15 minutes, or until the fries reach your desired level of crispiness
5. Remove the fries from the grill to a serving bowl, and toss with parsley. Serve with the chipotle ketchup for dipping.

Romaine Salad with Bacon

Prep time: 5 minutes | Cook time: 20 minutes | Serves 2

Salad:

- 1 romaine lettuce heart, cut in half
- 1 teaspoon olive oil
- Salt and freshly ground black pepper, to taste
- 2 teaspoons grated Parmesan cheese
- 6 slices cooked bacon, crumbled Dressing:
- ¼ cup milk
- 2 teaspoons blue cheese
- 2 teaspoons mayonnaise
- Salt and pepper, to taste Garlic powder, to taste

1. When ready to cook, set wood pellet grill temperature to 450°F (232°C) and preheat, lid closed for 15 minutes.
2. Drizzle the olive oil over both faces of the romaine. Season lettuce with salt, pepper, and Parmesan cheese.
3. Lay the romaine lettuce, face-down, on the grill and cook for 2 minutes.
4. Remove romaine from grill to a salad bowl. Make the dressing by mixing the blue cheese, mayonnaise, and milk in a small bowl. Season to taste with a little salt, pepper, and garlic powder.
5. Add the bacon to the salad bowl with romaine and pour over the dressing. Toss well and serve immediately.

Bacon & Jalapenos

Prep time: 15 minutes | Cook time: 1 hour | Serves 4

- 12 medium jalapeño
- 8 ounces (227 g) cream cheese, softened
- 2 tablespoons Traeger Pork & Poultry Rub
- 1 cup grated cheese
- 6 slices bacon, cut in half

1. When ready to cook, set wood pellet grill temperature to 180°F (82°C) and preheat, lid closed for 15 minutes. For optimal flavor, use Super Smoke if available.
2. Slice the jalapeños in half lengthwise. Scrape out any seeds and ribs with a small spoon or paring knife. In a bowl, stir together softened cream cheese with Traeger Pork & Poultry rub and grated cheese. Spoon the mixture into each jalapeño half. Wrap with bacon and secure with a toothpick.
3. Place the jalapeños on a rimmed baking sheet. Place on the grill and smoke for 30 minutes.
4. Increase the grill temperature to 375°F (191°C) and cook for an additional 30 minutes, or until bacon is cooked to desired doneness.
5. Serve warm.

Creamy Mashed Red Potatoes

Prep time: 15 minutes | Cook time: 40 minutes | Serves 4

- 8 large red potatoes
- Salt and black pepper, to taste
- ½ cup heavy cream
- ¼ cup butter, softened

1. When ready to cook, set temperature to 180°F (82°C) and preheat, lid closed for 15 minutes.
2. Slice red potatoes in half lengthwise, then cut in half again to make quarters. Season potatoes with salt and pepper.
3. Increase the heat to High and preheat. Once the grill is hot, place the potatoes directly on the grill. Every 15 minutes flip the potatoes to ensure all sides get color. Continue to do this until potatoes are fork-tender.
4. When tender, mash potatoes with heavy cream, butter, salt, and pepper to taste. Serve immediately.

Herb-Infused Riced Potatoes

Prep time: 20 minutes | Cook time: 1 hour | Serves 6

- 2½ pounds (1.1 kg) russet potatoes, peeled and cut into 1-inch cubes
- 1½ cups water
- 1 cup heavy cream
- 6 sage leaves
- 3 thyme sprigs
- 2 rosemary sprigs
- 2 tablespoons thyme leaves
- 6 peppercorns
- 2 garlic cloves
- 2 butter, sticks
- Salt and ground black pepper, to taste

1. When ready to cook, set wood pellet grill temperature to 350°F (177°C) and preheat, lid closed for 15 minutes.
2. Place the potatoes in a heatproof dish with water, cover and cook for 1 hour or until fork-tender.
3. Meanwhile, combine the heavy cream with the herbs, peppercorns, and garlic cloves in a small saucepan.
4. Place on the grill, cover, and allow to steep for 15 minutes. Strain the cream through a sieve to remove the herbs and garlic, place back in the saucepan and keep warm on the stove.
5. Drain and using a potato ricer, rice the potatoes back into the large stockpot. Slowly pour in two-thirds of the cream, then stir in 1 stick of the butter and 1 tablespoon of salt. Continue to add more cream, butter and salt to reach your desired consistency.
6. Serve immediately.

roasted Green Beans and Bacon

Prep time: 15 minutes | Cook time: 20 minutes | Serves 4

- 1½ pounds (680 g) fresh green beans
- 4 strips bacon, cut into small pieces
- 4 tablespoons extra-virgin olive oil
- 2 clove garlic, minced
- 1 teaspoon kosher salt

1. When ready to cook, set T wood pellet grill temperature to High and preheat, lid closed for 15 minutes.
2. Toss all ingredients together and spread out evenly on a sheet tray.
3. Place the tray directly on the grill and roast until the bacon is crispy and beans are lightly browned, about 20 minutes. Serve hot.

Grilled Peach and Tomato Salsa

Prep time: 5 minutes | Cook time: 8 to 10 minutes | Serves 6

- 6 peaches, halved
- 3 tomatoes, halved
- 2 jalapeños
- 2 green onions
- 2 cloves garlic
- ½ cup cilantro
- 5 teaspoons apple cider vinegar
- 1 teaspoon lime juice
- ½ teaspoon salt
- ¼ teaspoon black pepper

1. When ready to cook, set wood pellet grill temperature to 375°F (191°C) and preheat, lid closed for 15 minutes.
2. Place the peaches, tomatoes, and jalapeños on the grill grate. Close the lid and roast for 8 to 10 minutes, or until the skin has split and the tomatoes and jalapeños have blistered.
3. Remove from the grill and let rest for 5 minutes, or until the fruit can be easily handled.
4. Remove the skin from the peaches and tomatoes. Remove the skin, stems, and seeds from the jalapeños.
5. In a food processor, place the peeled peaches, tomatoes, jalapeños along with the green onions and pulse until coarsely chopped.
6. Add all the remaining ingredients and pulse until it reaches the desired consistency.
7. Serve immediately or stored in sealed jars in the refrigerator for up to 1 week.

Vinegary Rotini Salad

Prep time: 10 minutes | Cook time: 18 to 20 minutes | Serves 8

Salad:
- 1 pound (454 g) salami
- 8 ounces (227 g) Mozzarella cheese
- 1 red onion, diced
- 1 jar roasted red peppers, sliced
- 3 jarred pepperoncini peppers, thinly sliced
- 3 cups sliced cherry tomatoes
- ¾ cup black olives
- ¼ cup chopped flat-leaf parsley
- 1 pound (454 g) rotini pasta Vinaigrette:
- 3 cloves garlic, minced
- ½ cup extra-virgin olive oil
- ½ cup red wine vinegar
- 1 tablespoon Italian seasoning
- 1 tablespoon honey
- Kosher salt, to taste
- Black pepper, to taste

1. When ready to cook, set wood pellet grill temperature to 180°F (82°C) and preheat, lid closed for 15 minutes.
2. Put all the salad ingredients, except for the pasta, on a sheet tray. Place the tray on the grill and smoke for 10 minutes. Remove from the grill and set aside.
3. Bring a large pot of salted water to a boil over high heat and cook the pasta for 8 to 10 minutes, or until al dente.
4. Meanwhile, stir together all the ingredients for the vinaigrette in a small bowl and set aside.
5. Drain the pasta and rinse under cold water. Transfer the pasta to a large mixing bowl.

6. Chop all the salad ingredients and transfer to the mixing bowl with the pasta. Spread the vinaigrette over the top and toss to coat well.
7. Cover in plastic and set in the refrigerator for 30 minutes before serving.
8. Serve chilled.

Mini Veggie Quiches

Prep time: 10 minutes | Cook time: 26 to 28 minutes | Serves 8

- 1 tablespoon extra-virgin olive oil
- ½ yellow onion, diced
- 3 cups fresh spinach
- 10 eggs
- 4 ounces (113 g) shredded Cheddar cheese
- ¼ cup fresh basil
- 1 teaspoon kosher salt
- ½ teaspoon black pepper
- Cooking spray

1. Spritz a 12-cup muffin tin with cooking spray. Set aside.
2. Heat the oil in a skillet over medium heat. Add the onion and cook for about 7 minutes, or until tender, stirring frequently. Add the spinach and cook for 1 more minute, or until wilted.
3. Transfer the cooked veggies to a clean work surface to cool, then chop the veggies.
4. When ready to cook, set wood pellet grill temperature to 350°F (177°C) and preheat, lid closed for 15 minutes.
5. In a large bowl, whisk the eggs until frothy. Stir in the cooled veggies along with the remaining ingredients. Divide the egg mixture evenly among the muffin cups.
6. Place the muffin tin on the grill and bake for 18 to 20 minutes, or until the eggs have puffed up, are set, and are beginning to brown.
7. Serve immediately, or let cool on a wire rack, then refrigerate in a sealed container for up to 4 days.

Smoked Chickpeas with Roasted Veggies

Prep time: 15 minutes | Cook time: 30 to 40 minutes | Serves 4

- 1½ cups chickpeas, drained and rinsed
- ⅓ cup tahini
- 4 tablespoons lemon juice
- 2 tablespoons extra-virgin olive oil
- 1 tablespoon minced garlic,
- 1 teaspoon salt
- 2 cups cauliflower, cut into florets
- 2 cups butternut squash
- 2 cups fresh Brussels sprouts
- 2 whole portobello mushrooms
- 1 red onion, sliced
- 4 tablespoons extra-virgin olive oil

1. When ready to cook, set wood pellet grill temperature to 180°F (82°C) and preheat, lid closed for 15 minutes.
2. Spread the chickpeas on a sheet tray. Place the tray on the grill grate and smoke for 15 to 20 minutes.
3. In a food processor, combine the smoked chickpeas, tahini, lemon juice, olive oil, garlic and salt. Pulse until mixed well but not completely smooth. Transfer to a bowl and set aside.
4. Increase wood pellet grill temperature to High and preheat, lid closed for 15 minutes.
5. Toss the veggies with the olive oil to coat and spread on a sheet tray. Place the sheet tray on the grill and roast for 15 to 20 minutes, or until lightly browned and cooked through.
6. Transfer the mashed chickpeas to a serving platter and top with the roasted veggies.
7. Serve immediately.

Sweet Potatoes with Marshmallow Sauce

Prep time: 5 minutes | Cook time: 1 hour 5 minutes | Serves 4

- 4 large sweet potatoes
- 8 tablespoons sliced butter
- ½ cup brown sugar
- ¼ teaspoon ground nutmeg
- Salt, to taste
- Marshmallow Sauce:
- 1 cup mini marshmallows
- 1 tablespoon melted butter

1. When ready to cook, set the T wood pellet grill to High and preheat, lid closed for 15 minutes.
2. Place a sweet potato on a clean work surface horizontally between the handles of 2 wooden spoons. Slice the potato into thin slices, leaving ¼ inch at the bottom unsliced. The spoon handles will prevent slicing the potato all the way through. Repeat with the remaining potatoes.
3. Insert a thin slice of butter between the potato slices. Sprinkle with the brown sugar, nutmeg and salt.
4. Arrange the potatoes on a sheet tray. Place the tray on the grill and bake for 1 hour, or until cooked through and crispy on top.
5. Meanwhile, make the marshmallow sauce: Combine the mini marshmallows and melted butter in a saucepan over medium heat, until the mallows are melted and creamy.
6. When the potatoes are baked, add a dollop of marshmallow sauce to the top of each potato.
7. Return the tray to the grill and bake for an additional 5 minutes, or until the marshmallows have melted.
8. Remove from the oven. Let cool for 5 minutes before serving.

Crispy Sweet Potato Fries

Prep time: 5 minutes | Cook time: 20 to 30 minutes | Serves 4

- 4 sweet potatoes, peeled and cut into sticks
- 3 tablespoons extra-virgin olive oil
- 1 tablespoon salt
- 1 teaspoon black pepper
- 1 cup mayonnaise
- 2 chipotle peppers in adobe sauce
- 2 limes, juiced

1. When ready to cook, set the wood pellet grill to High and preheat, lid closed for 15 minutes.
2. In a medium bowl, toss together the sweet potatoes, olive oil, salt and pepper to coat. Transfer to a sheet pan.
3. Place the sheet pan on the grill grate and roast for 20 to 30 minutes, or until the potatoes are brown and crispy, stirring occasionally.
4. Meanwhile, combine the mayonnaise, chipotle peppers and lime juice in a blender and pulse until smooth.
5. Serve the sweet potato fries with the mayonnaise sauce.

PERFECT SWEET ENDING TO A BBQ

Grilled Pound Cake with Fruit Dressing

Preparation Time: 20 Minutes

Cooking Time: 50 Minutes

Servings: 12

Ingredients:

- 1 buttermilk pound cake, sliced into 3/4-inch slices
- 1/8 cup butter, melted
- 1.1/2 cup whipped cream
- 1/2 cup blueberries
- 1/2 cup raspberries
- 1/2 cup strawberries, sliced

Directions:

1. Preheat pellet grill to 400°F. Turn your smoke setting to high, if applicable.

2. Brush both sides of each pound cake slice with melted butter.

3. Place directly on the grill grate and cook for 5 minutes per side. Turn 90° halfway through cooking each side of the cake for checkered grill marks.

4. You can cook a couple of minutes longer if you prefer deeper grill marks and smoky flavor.

5. Remove pound cake slices from the grill and allow it to cool on a plate.

6. Top slices with whipped cream, blueberries, raspberries, and sliced strawberries as desired. Serve and enjoy!

Grilled Pineapple with Chocolate Sauce

Preparation Time: 10 Minutes

Cooking Time: 25 Minutes

Servings: 8

Ingredients:

- 1 pineapple

- 8 oz bittersweet chocolate chips

- 1/2 cup spiced rum

- 1/2 cup whipping cream

- 2 tbsp light brown sugar

Directions:

1. Preheat pellet grill to 400°F.

2. De-skin the pineapple and slice pineapple into 1 in cubes.

3. In a saucepan, combine chocolate chips. When chips begin to melt, add rum to the saucepan. Continue to stir until combined, then add a splash of the pineapple's juice.

4. Add in whipping cream and continue to stir the mixture. Once the sauce is smooth and thickening, lower heat to simmer to keep warm.

5. Thread pineapple cubes onto skewers. Sprinkle skewers with brown sugar.

6. Place skewers on the grill grate. Grill for about 5 minutes per side, or until grill marks begin to develop.

7. Remove skewers from grill and allow to rest on a plate for about 5 minutes. Serve alongside warm chocolate sauce for dipping.

Nectarine and Nutella Sundae

Preparation Time: 10 Minutes

Cooking Time: 25 Minutes

Servings: 4

Ingredients:

- 2nectarines, halved and pitted
- 2tsp honey
- 4tbsp Nutella
- 4scoops vanilla ice cream
- 1/4 cup pecans, chopped
- Whipped cream, to top
- 4cherries, to top

Directions:

1. Preheat pellet grill to 400°F.

2. Slice nectarines in half and remove the pits.

3. Brush the inside (cut side) of each nectarine half with honey.

4. Place nectarines directly on the grill grate, cut side down. Cook for 5-6 minutes, or until grill marks develop.

5. Flip nectarines and cook on the other side for about 2 minutes.

6. Remove nectarines from the grill and allow it to cool.

7. Fill the pit cavity on each nectarine half with 1 tbsp Nutella.

8.   Place 1 scoop of ice cream on top of Nutella. Top with whipped cream, cherries, and sprinkle chopped pecans. Serve and enjoy!

Cinnamon Sugar Donut Holes

Preparation Time: 10 Minutes

Cooking Time: 35 Minutes

Servings: 4

Ingredients:

- 1/2 cup flour
- 1tbsp cornstarch
- 1/2 tsp baking powder
- 1/8 tsp baking soda
- 1/8 tsp ground cinnamon
- 1/2 tsp kosher salt
- 1/4 cup buttermilk
- 1/4 cup sugar
- 11/2 tbsp butter, melted
- 1egg
- 1/2 tsp vanilla
- Topping
- 2tbsp sugar
- 1tbsp sugar
- 1tsp ground cinnamon

Directions:

1. Preheat pellet grill to 350°F.

2. In a medium bowl, combine flour, cornstarch, baking powder, baking soda, ground cinnamon, and kosher salt. Whisk to combine.

3. In a separate bowl, combine buttermilk, sugar, melted butter, egg, and vanilla. Whisk until the egg is thoroughly combined.

4. Pour wet mixture into the flour mixture and stir. Stir just until combined, careful not to overwork the mixture.

5. Spray mini muffin tin with cooking spray.

6. Spoon 1 tbsp of donut mixture into each mini muffin hole.

7. Place the tin on the pellet grill grate and bake for about 18 minutes, or until a toothpick can come out clean.

8. Remove muffin tin from the grill and let rest for about 5 minutes.

9. In a small bowl, combine 1 tbsp sugar and 1 tsp ground cinnamon.

10. Melt 2 tbsp of butter in a glass dish. Dip each donut hole in the melted butter, then mix and toss with cinnamon sugar. Place completed donut holes on a plate to serve.

Pellet Grill Chocolate Chip Cookies

Preparation Time: 20 Minutes

Cooking Time: 45 Minutes

Servings: 12

Ingredients:

- 1cup salted butter, softened
- 1cup of sugar
- 1cup light brown sugar
- 2tsp vanilla extract
- 2large eggs
- 3cups all-purpose flour
- 1tsp baking soda
- 1/2 tsp baking powder
- 1tsp natural sea salt
- 2cups semi-sweet chocolate chips, or chunks

Directions:

1. Preheat pellet grill to 375°F.

2. Line a large baking sheet with parchment paper and set aside.

3. In a medium bowl, mix flour, baking soda, salt, and baking powder. Once combined, set aside.

4. In stand mixer bowl, combine butter, white sugar, and brown sugar until combined. Beat in eggs and vanilla. Beat until fluffy.

5. Mix in dry ingredients, continue to stir until combined.

6. Add chocolate chips and mix thoroughly.

7. Roll 3 tbsp of dough at a time into balls and place them on your cookie sheet. Evenly space them apart, with about 2-3 inches in between each ball.

8. Place cookie sheet directly on the grill grate and bake for 20-25 minutes until the cookies' outside is slightly browned.

9. Remove from grill and allow to rest for 10 minutes. Serve and enjoy!

Delicious Donuts on a Grill

Preparation Time: 5 Minutes

Cooking Time: 10 Minutes

Servings: 6

Ingredients:

- 1-1/2 cups sugar, powdered
- 1/3 cup whole milk
- 1/2 teaspoon vanilla extract
- 16 ounces of biscuit dough, prepared
- Oil spray, for greasing
- 1cup chocolate sprinkles, for sprinkling

Directions:

1. Take a medium bowl and mix sugar, milk, and vanilla extract.
2. Combine well to create a glaze.
3. Set the glaze aside for further use.
4. Place the dough onto the flat, clean surface.
5. Flat the dough with a rolling pin.
6. Use a ring mold, about an inch, and cut the hole in the center of each round dough.
7. Place the dough on a plate and refrigerate for 10 minutes.
8. Open the grill and install the grill grate inside it.
9. Close the hood.

10. Now, select the grill from the menu, and set the temperature to medium.

11. Set the time to 6 minutes.

12. Select start and begin preheating.

13. Remove the dough from the refrigerator and coat it with cooking spray from both sides.

14. When the unit beeps, the grill is preheated; place the adjustable amount of dough on the grill grate.

15. Close the hood, and cook for 3 minutes.

16. After 3 minutes, remove donuts and place the remaining dough inside.

17. Cook for 3 minutes.

18. Once all the donuts are ready, sprinkle chocolate sprinkles on top.

19. Enjoy.

Smoked Pumpkin Pie

Preparation Time: 10 Minutes

Cooking Time: 50 Minutes

Servings: 8

Ingredients:

- 1tbsp cinnamon
- 1-1/2 tbsp pumpkin pie spice
- 15oz can pumpkin
- 14oz can sweetened condensed milk
- 2beaten eggs
- 1unbaked pie shell
- Topping: whipped cream

Directions:

2. Preheat your smoker to 325oF.

3. Place a baking sheet, rimmed, on the smoker upside down, or use a cake pan.

4. Combine all your ingredients in a bowl, large, except the pie shell, then pour the mixture into a pie crust.

5. Place the pie on the baking sheet and smoke for about 50-60 minutes until a knife comes out clean when inserted. Make sure the center is set.

6. Remove and cool for about 2 hours or refrigerate overnight.

7. Serve with a whipped cream dollop and enjoy it!

– THE –

EST. **OLD** 1999
**TEXAS
PITMASTER**

TRAVIS COUNTY

THE OLD TEXAS PITMASTER

EST. 1999

TRAVIS COUNTY

www.ingramcontent.com/pod-product-compliance
Lightning Source LLC
Chambersburg PA
CBHW071856160426
43209CB00005B/1076